Edmund Walker

History of Banking in Canada

Edmund Walker

History of Banking in Canada

ISBN/EAN: 9783743313767

Manufactured in Europe, USA, Canada, Australia, Japa

Cover: Foto ©ninafisch / pixelio.de

Manufactured and distributed by brebook publishing software
(www.brebook.com)

Edmund Walker

History of Banking in Canada

A HISTORY OF
BANKING IN CANADA

—BY—

B. E. WALKER

General Manager of the Canadian Bank of Commerce

Reprinted from "A History of Banking in All Nations," by permission of the publishers, The Journal of Commerce and Commercial Bulletin, New York.

Toronto, Canada
1899

AUTHOR'S PREFACE

ALTHOUGH it is only since the customary decennial revision of the Bank Act in 1890 that the Canadian system of banking can be said to have been a subject of interest to any but the citizens of that country, the history of currency and banking in Canada is of considerable antiquity, dating as it does from the early part of the seventeenth century. And from the point of view of development, it has the advantage of beginning with the simplest conditions of barter, followed by a currency limited to moose and beaver skins, and passing by intelligible stages to a condition of sufficient perfection to be worthy of consideration as one of the half-dozen best systems in the world.

But the total wealth involved in Canadian banking is only about $320,000,000, a sum very small when compared with the great trading nations, such as Great Britain, France, Germany, and the United States. In its early stages, indeed, the actual money involved was so trifling that it seems scarcely worth while to record such facts in history. Principles, however, are more important than the range of their application, and in the history of the development of Canada, whether we consider banking, or representative government, or any other important branch of society, its people have always shown a strong disposition to discuss the reasons of things, whether the application at the moment was important or not. If there are any general principles lying at the foundation of banking they will assert themselves as well in a small volume of business as in the transactions of a great nation.

In attempting to set forth the history of the currency and banking of Canada, up to the last revision of the Bank Act, the facts fall naturally into the following groups:

1608–1760, New France. Card money and other paper issues · · 1685 1719 1729–1749, and 1750–1760.

1760–1791, British occupation. Country without paper money. Coins of several countries a legal tender.

1791–1812, Representative government established in 1791, but attempts to obtain charters for banks of issue unsuccessful.

1812–1817, Paper money issued by the Army-bill Office.

1817–1867, Joint-stock banks under provincial charters.

1867–1890, Dominion of Canada. Charters issued by the Federal instead of Provincial Government.

The writer has endeavored to deal with these periods as succinctly as possible in order that he might write more fully regarding the nature of the act now in force.

The space at disposal does not permit of the present work being more than a study of the development and principles of Canadian banking, but care has been taken to make such references as may enable the reader to obtain access to histories which deal fully with the various periods, and present in detail all important incidents. The writer has also been careful to avoid the mention by name of banks or individuals, excepting so far as such a course was necessary in writing a mere history of development.

A HISTORY OF BANKING IN CANADA

CHAPTER I

CURRENCY EXPEDIENTS

1608-1760, CARD MONEY OF NEW FRANCE; 1760-1812, RESORT TO FOREIGN COIN; 1812-1817, ARMY-BILL ISSUES

NO theory supported the issue in 1685 of the first paper money in Canada. The little communities at Quebec, Three Rivers, and Montreal had existed for three-quarters of a century, presenting the strange contrast to their present industrial habits of a distinctly mediæval civilization, at war, externally, with the savage Indian and the primeval condition of nature, and—when for a moment the Iroquois had disappeared—internally, about petty questions of political and social precedence; as to whether brandy should be sold to the friendly Indians who had furs to exchange; to what extent the unhappy colonist should be bled by the so-called Trading Company, to which an ignorant king had given a monopoly of both export and import trade, and by priests illegally trading in furs, etc. While religious zealots in France saw only the opportunity to convert Indians for the glory of God, civil and military servants in the colony and the Government in France actually exacted tribute from New France. But had there been before the colonists merely the problems of food and clothing and such public improvements as necessity demanded, they would doubtless have been unable, as all new countries now are, to export enough to pay for their imports. And so, such coined money as came to the colony, chiefly for military and civil expenditure by the Government, quickly returned, and for many years beaver-skins, the most important product, served as the chief money, other furs being also either recognized standards of value or readily exchangeable by barter, while a decree was not necessary to make brandy a most satisfactory medium of exchange with the Indians.

EARLIEST MONETARY EXPEDIENTS

The difficulty was not always, however, with the trapper and agriculturist in finding a satisfactory exchange for the imported goods sold by the merchant. The colony was so poor that the products often had to be exported to France and sold before the necessary supplies could be sent in return. To enable trade to be carried on with some degree of comfort, the French West Indies Company, which had the control of the trade of Canada in 1670, brought about the issue of a coinage of subsidiary silver and copper for use in the French colonies; but even these change-making coins returned at once to France.

The next expedient was a decree, in 1672, for the avowed purpose of keeping coined money in Canada, according to which the coinage of the colonies and of France was to be taken at one-third more than the face value. This did no good whatever, and in addition to enabling the Trading Company to exact unfair profits, it created two species of money, the French standard (*monnoye de france* or *livre tournois*) and the colonial standard (*monnoye du pays*). In 1674 another decree annulled the action of 1672 regarding the difference between the face value and the value in trade of the coinage, but the custom of paying for furs and similar merchandise by giving twenty-five per cent. less in coined money remained until 1719.

All expedients having failed to retain the one satisfactory kind of currency, in 1679 the farmers who were now evidently making themselves felt politically, were permitted, for a period of three months, to pay their debts in wheat at the fixed rate of four livres per minot (three French bushels). And, in like manner, about 1684, moose-skins were a legal tender in paying debts already incurred, at rates named by the authorities

CARD MONEY

For a few years previous to 1685, the Government of France had supplied in advance the money and goods necessary for the support of their civil and military establishments in Canada, but for this year these failed to arrive. The Intendant, Jacques de Meuilles, evidently more fertile in resources than his predecessors, after having spent all the money he had or could borrow, resorted to the following expedient: Instead of silver he paid soldiers by notes made of playing-cards cut in four pieces. The denominations of these were four francs, forty sols, and fifteen sols, with which three kinds he could pay a soldier's monthly wages. He ordered the people to accept, and personally undertook to redeem them.* They are said to have borne simply the written amount of their value in *monnoye du pays*, the signatures of the Intendant and the Clerk of the Treasury, and the crowned fleur-de-lis impressed in wax. The new currency must have solved many of the difficulties of trade, and we are not surprised to learn that thereafter France made no effort to send supplies a year in advance, while resort to this *monnoye de carte* became the recognized means of carrying the debts of the Colonial Government over the year, or until the ships arrived in the autumn from France. Subsequent issues appear to have been very carefully guarded. The Governor and the Intendant, for their respective disbursements, might employ the aid of card money, and the notes, therefore, bore the signature of the Governor, the Intendant, and the Clerk of the Treasury. After the necessary decree establishing the legal-tender quality of each issue, the Clerk of the Treasury receipted for them in the same manner as for actual remittances from France. Until 1709 the cards for the year were redeemed in specie when the ships arrived, or, if preferred by the holder, drafts on the

*The foregoing statement is true.

French Treasury could be obtained at any time during the year. The success of the expedient, thus far, was not unmerited, and the currency cannot be regarded as entirely unsound, since it was merely a series of issues limited to the amount of the annual remittance and redeemed in specie on arrival.

In 1709, however, in consequence of the bankrupt condition of France, owing to European wars, drafts already given in exchange for the cards were refused and the regular remittances discontinued. The legitimate basis of the card money was now gone, while the necessity for its issue was greatly increased. Instead of issues restricted to the amount of a year's expenditure, the unredeemed cards of one year were succeeded by those of another until the volume increased fourfold, the total outstanding in 1714 being computed at 2,120,000 livres, while the population was only 19,000. At this time it was decided to redeem them gradually at one-half, and during the ensuing three years bills of exchange were drawn on the French Treasury for five-sevenths of the above amount. But the French Treasury did not resume remittances for current expenditures, and for this purpose new issues were necessary, so that by 1717 the total outstanding was 1,730,000 livres. In this year, however, arrangements were made not only for the redemption of all cards at one-half, but for the cessation of future issues, and the return to the currency standard of old France in exchange for the *monnoye du pays*.

RETURN TO COIN MONEY—THEN A RELAPSE TO CARDS

By 1719 the redemption of the card money was accomplished, and for about ten years, during which period there were many unsuccessful efforts to interfere by decrees with the natural course of things, coined money was the only currency—always scarce, and with a persistent tendency to return to old France. By 1728, we find the Governor suggesting a new issue of card money as the only relief, and early in 1729 the King, by ordinance and in accordance with the wish of the colonists, created again for Canada a card currency. The new cards were limited to 400,000 livres, were issued in seven convenient denominations, were a legal tender, receivable for all goods sold by Government, and were redeemable by drafts on the French Treasury. This issue was thus surrounded by careful regulations, but was distinctly a *fiat* currency, to be reissued as soon as redeemed—a permanent loan to the Government. It was not actually redeemable in specie, although as long as the volume was restricted, redemption by drafts on the French Treasury was practically quite as satisfactory. But the population had increased to 30,000, and the volume of currency being deemed quite insufficient, the King, who now controlled the issue, was induced in 1733 to increase the limit to 600,000 livres. In 1742 it was again increased to 720,000 livres, and in 1749 to 1,000,000 livres. Thus far the issues were promptly redeemed by drafts on the French Treasury, and from history we do not learn that anything but good arose from this reasonable use of paper money.

From this time until the capitulation in 1760, the colony was constantly increasing its expenditures in order to carry on its struggle with the English colonies. The annual expenditure, which in 1749 was less than 2,000,000 livres, by 1758 reached nearly 28,000,000 livres, and during the seven years 1749 to 1755 inclusive, the exports did not amount to thirty per cent. of the imports. The receipts of money from France were quite insufficient for such unusual expenditure, and, to the high prices attendant upon the over-issue of paper money to which we are about to refer, there was added the cost to the Public Treasury of the corrupt extravagance of the Intendant Bigot.

BIGOT'S DUE-BILL CURRENCY (ORDONNANCES)

The limit of 1,000,000 livres being too small and the issue of cards being illegal, unless sanctioned by the King, Bigot resorted to a new species of currency. He issued printed due-bills called *ordonnances* for even sums from 20 sols to 100 livres. The notes were signed by the Intendant only, and there was practically no limit except the ability of the community to absorb such issues. They were not redeemable in specie, but were redeemable in card money under certain circumstances. In the autumn the moneys and credit supplied by the French Treasury were available to redeem the authorized card money. This card money, being reissuable as long as the limit of 1,000,000 livres was not exceeded, was used to redeem as far as it would go the ordonnances of Bigot, and for such portion as could not be redeemed by card money a third species of obligation was issued in the shape of bonds of the Canadian Treasury, payable in one year in card money.

A disparity in value was thus created between the card money and the ordonnances, and in 1754 this was removed by taking away from the former any priority in the conversion into bills of exchange on the French Treasury, both cards and ordonnances being redeemed on the same level, as far as redemption was effected at all. Instead of raising the ordonnances to the level of the cards, this measure reduced the latter to the level of the former. In 1756 an attempt was made to fix at twenty-five per cent. the depreciation of the paper currency relatively to specie. But the pressure of war upon France in several parts of the world made financial reform impossible, and matters grew steadily worse, little restraint thereafter being attempted in the volume of paper money emitted. The drafts on the French Treasury for 1758 and 1759 were not paid, and cards and ordonnances fell to a discount of sixty to seventy per cent. At the capitulation in 1760, there were outstanding 34,000,000 livres of ordonnances and 7,000,000 livres of cards and Treasury bonds, while other evidences of debt brought the total liability of the Canadian colony up to 80,000,000 livres.

The new British rulers insisted upon a settlement by France of such evidences of debt as were held by the Canadian people, and notwithstanding the bankrupt condition of France, this was brought about by a convention, signed in 1766, under which bills of exchange and anything subject to redemption in them were paid at fifty per cent. of the face value, while ordonnances and other forms of debt were paid at twenty-five per cent., and there was added to this a bonus on the whole settlement of 3,000,000 livres. Payment was made, however, in French public securities, which in May,

1766, sold as low as 74, and which rapidly declined in a few years until they became almost completely worthless.*

CURRENCY UNDER BRITISH RULE

One of the first acts of the new British Governor was to warn the people not to take the paper issues of the old régime, and as early as 1764 we find importations of Mexican dollars with which to pay the troops. At the same time gold and silver coins of England, Spain, Portugal, France and Germany were in circulation, and these miscellaneous coins furnished the only currency. It was thought necessary that the money of account should now bear English names in addition to French, but with as little alteration in the actual significance as possible. It was therefore decided that from and after January 1, 1765, the livre should be estimated at the same value as a shilling of the new Canadian currency, and that six livres or shillings should be the equivalent of a dollar. Accounts were to be kept in pounds, shillings, and pence, Canada currency (not sterling), and the same law made legal tender, and settled the value in pounds, shillings, and pence, Canada currency, of the various gold, silver, and copper coins already referred to, which formed the actual currency. In 1777, a new law was passed changing all these values on the basis of five Canadian shillings instead of six for the Spanish or Mexican silver dollar, and this established the Canadian currency which existed until the decimal system, expressed in dollars and cents, was adopted.

But the silver coins of the various countries were, because of their worn condition and for other reasons, unsuitable for shipment abroad, and therefore gold coins were sought for this purpose, and complaints as to the unsatisfactory state of the currency were still frequent. In 1791, constitutional government, instead of government by a Governor and Council of State, was conferred on Canada, the country being divided

*The first monograph on the card money in England with which I am acquainted is that of the late James Stevenson, "Currency, with Reference to Card Money in Canada During the French Domination." Transactions Literary and Historical Society of Quebec, 1876. To it is appended a copy of the convention of 1766 for the liquidation of the Canada paper money. A much more exhaustive monograph appeared in 1894 by Mr. R. M. Breckenridge, entitled "The Paper Currencies of New France." *Journal of Political Economy*, Chicago. In it references are made to all French and English sources of information.

into Upper Canada (now Ontario) and Lower Canada (Quebec). The Parliament of Quebec in 1795 passed an act increasing the value of the gold coins which were a legal tender, hoping thereby to prevent their export, and requiring payments in excess of £50 to be made in gold. The new law also declared that the new American dollar should be counted like the Spanish and Mexican, at five shillings, and all other silver coins likewise remained unchanged. In 1796 Upper Canada passed a similar act. Another act was passed in 1808 still further enhancing the value of some of the foreign gold pieces; but, without a coined currency or a banking system, no satisfactory solution could be found.

Joint-stock banks of the modern type—that is banks of issue, deposit and discount—had been established in the United States, despite the bankruptcy of all legal-tender issues, colonial and "Continental." In 1781, the Bank of North America of Philadelphia, still flourishing, was chartered. In 1784, Massachusetts chartered a bank. In 1791, the first United States Bank began its career, and thereafter many banks sprang into existence.

[redacted]

The merchants of Canada were not blind to what was going on elsewhere. Montreal had already become more important commercially than Quebec, and on October 18, 1792, the "Official Gazette" contained an announcement looking to the establishment in the former city of a bank under the name of the "Canada Banking Company." It was proposed that the Company should transact the business "usually done by similar establishments," viz., to receive deposits, issue notes, discount bills, and keep cash accounts with customers. It was further proposed to open branches—"to extend the operations of the bank to every part of the two provinces where an agent may be judged necessary." The scheme, although supported by the leading merchants, failed in its main purpose; the result being a private bank without the legislative authority to issue notes.* Canada was enjoying

*As a matter of fact it did issue notes, specimens of which the writer has seen, but they doubtless had a very limited use.

its first year of constitutional government, and although the author has seen no record of Parliamentary debate, we must suppose that such an important proposal was fully discussed in one way or another before it was abandoned. One able writer has attributed the lack of success to the disturbed state of Europe and political apprehension of trouble; but we must remember that in 1792 there were many living who had personally experienced loss by the repudiated paper currency of the old régime, while opponents of the plan might cite the universal bankruptcy at the time of the revolution of all paper issues in the United States. It was therefore only natural that the right of issue should have been withheld. The merchant of Canada at that time suffered greatly through the confusion arising from a currency consisting of the coins of other countries, but he hesitated to abandon this position of comparative safety for one which must have seemed to him to be full of known as well as unknown dangers. The effort to issue bank notes was not renewed until 1807, this time at Quebec, but again without success.

In 1808, citizens of both Montreal and Quebec asked Parliament to grant a charter for the "Canada Bank," and after reference to a committee a bill was introduced. The capital of the bank was to be £250,000 currency ($1,000,000), divided in shares of £25 currency ($100). There were to be twenty-four directors elected by the shareholders, one-half to attend to the affairs of the bank at Montreal, and the other half at Quebec, these being the two most important offices. The directors were to elect the president and vice-president. But the charter was refused. In the Legislature it was argued that the creation of a bank with power of issue would drive out all specie, would foster speculation founded on imaginary capital, that the people were too ignorant to understand the denominations of notes or guard against counterfeits, etc.

RESORT TO ARMY BILLS AS CURRENCY

In 1812 Canada was suddenly plunged into war with the United States. War was declared on the 19th of June, and on July 16th the Parliament of Lower Canada met and remained in session until August 1st. During this time they passed an act to meet the financial requirements of the army. It was very elaborate in details and bore evidence of a strong desire to preserve the rights of the public as far as compatible with the object of the issue. The features important from our point of view are :

1. The Governor, as Commander of the Army, was authorized to issue bills in suitable denominations, to be called "Army Bills," and to be limited in the aggregate to £250,000 currency. 2. Bills of $25 each and upwards to bear interest at four pence per hundred pounds per diem. 3. The principal of bills of $25 each and upwards to be payable, at the option of the Commander, in cash, or Government bills of exchange on London, at thirty days' sight, at the current rate of exchange. Upon such payment of principal the interest to be payable, at the option of the holder, in cash or army bills. 4. Within the prescribed limit of £250,000 currency, the Commander was empowered also to issue bills of $4 each, to be payable to the holder in cash on demand, and therefore not to bear interest. 5. All army bills to be issued as cash, *i. e.*, not sold at a discount or premium. 6. The current rate of exchange for bills on London to be established by a committee of five, named by the Governor, and to be advertised fortnightly. 7. No army bills to be reissued except those of $4 each. 8. The revenues of the province were pledged, in preference to all other claims, for the interest on the army bills. 9. Army bills, with interest accrued, were receivable by all collectors of Government dues. 10. Various regulations referring to arrest for debt, attachment, capias, etc., had the effect of making the army bills practically a legal tender. 11. On fourteen days' notice by authorities bills became redeemable and interest ceased. 12. At expiration of five years all notes became due and payable in cash out of moneys in the hands of the Receiver-General of the province. If such moneys were not sufficient, then out of first moneys received thereafter. Payment might be had at any time by bills of exchange on London, but this provision was made to enable the army bills to be held by Canadians as an investment.

13. During this period of five years no gold, silver, or copper coin, or "molten gold or silver in any shape or shapes whatever," were to be exported under penalty of forfeiture of the whole, and also of a fine levied upon the exporter of £100 currency, and double the value of the coin or metal exported. Permission to carry on the person £10, or a larger amount if authorized by the Governor.

On the passage of the act and the opening of the Army Bill Office, bills were issued of the denominations of $25, $50, $100 and $400, and evidently of $4 also. These were readily accepted by the people, and the issue was not only successful as an expedient of war finance, but was a boon to the commerce of the country, which had been struggling along with the mixed currency of foreign coins already mentioned. After the manner of war expenditures, however, the amount was insufficient, and another bill was passed at the next session of Parliament and assented to February 15, 1813, under which the aggregate of the issue was raised to £500,000 currency. Denominations of 1, 2, 8, 10, 12, 16 and 20 dollars were added to those already authorized, to be non-interest-bearing, in accordance with the provision of the first act. The total of non-interest-bearing notes, *i.e.*, notes of denominations smaller than $25, was, however, limited to £50,000 currency.

But the war did not come to an end, and in 1814 a third act was passed enlarging the limit to £1,500,000 currency. The only new provision of importance rearranged the issue of small notes in denominations of 1, 2, 3, 5 and 10 dollars non-interest-bearing, but payable like the larger denominations, by exchange on London, and required that as much as £100,000 currency and not more than £500,000 currency of the entire issue should be in these denominations. Holders of these smaller denominations could exchange them for interest-bearing issues. In the second and third acts the provisions cited in paragraphs 9 and 13 of the abstract of the first act were not extended to any issues beyond the first £250,000 currency. In February, 1815, the Parliament was about to pass another bill increasing the limit to £2,000,000 currency, when news arrived announcing the treaty of peace between

Great Britain and the United States signed at Ghent, December 24, 1814.

The public accounts show that on March 27, 1815, the entire amount of army bills outstanding was £1,249,996 currency. By December 4, 1815, this had been reduced to £396,778 currency, and by April 22, 1816, to £197,974 currency. The time originally set for the retirement of all army bills was August, 1817, but by various orders this was extended until December 24, 1820, at which time the Army Bill Office was closed, the entire issue of notes having been practically redeemed. Of the £1,300,000, or thereabouts, outstanding in 1815, only about £800,000 was in interest-bearing notes, while as much as £500,000 was in notes of change-making denominations not bearing interest. In view of this fact much credit was taken by the army officials for the low rate of interest which the issue, as a whole, cost the Home Government.

The elaborate nature of the various Army-bill Acts, the intelligent discussion at the time they were passed, and the criticisms in the press regarding the effect of the issues on the trade of the country, all show that the Canadian people held sound views on currency questions and were very much more intelligent than fifty years previously when the French card money was being redeemed. The provision by which the public could exchange notes of large denominations bearing interest for notes of small denominations not bearing interest, ensured a sufficient amount of currency for the trade of the country; while on the other hand, the reverse condition, under which non-interest-bearing notes could be exchanged for interest-bearing notes, ensured the redemption of all currency not required for trade purposes, by its conversion into what was practically an investment security. This quality of elasticity in the currency is very distinctly referred to in the contemporaneous discussions.*

* Readers desirous of studying more exhaustively the period during which the country was without paper money and the coins of several foreign countries were a legal tender should consult the second monograph by the late James Stevenson, entitled "The Currency of Canada after the Capitulation," Transactions of the Literary and Historical Society of Quebec, 1877; and for the army-bill issues the third historical monograph by the same gentleman, entitled "The War of 1812 in Connection with the Army-bill Act," published by W. Foster Brown & Co., Montreal, 1892.

CHAPTER II

1817–1841

BANKING UNDER JOINT-STOCK CHARTERS

LEGISLATION BY THE PROVINCES

EXPERIENCE OF TREASURY NOTES

WE are now approaching the period of joint-stock banking, and it will have been noticed that we have dealt with the currency history of only one portion of the present Dominion of Canada, that now known as the province of Quebec. In considering the conditions of banking preceding the confederation of the British North American provinces and territories, which took place in 1867, we shall have to deal with the portions of the present Dominion now known as Quebec, Ontario, Nova Scotia and New Brunswick, but before doing this it is necessary to refer briefly to the early conditions in Nova Scotia.

In 1801 an attempt was made in that province to obtain the monopoly of banking for a proposed company with a capital of £50,000 currency, but without success; and in 1811 an effort by the Halifax Committee of Trade to found a bank also failed. In 1812 the Treasury, however, made an issue of £12,000 currency of notes bearing interest at six per cent. and not reissuable. This was a simple and apparently harmless borrowing expedient, but, perhaps because of the absence of a sound bank of issue, the province went early astray. This issue was redeemed, but in 1813 it was followed by an issue of £20,000 currency *not* bearing interest and *reissuable.* From this year until confederation, in 1867, Nova Scotia never ceased to issue currency, and when its debts were assumed by the Dominion the total outstanding in this form amounted to £605,859. After 1812 the notes were not redeemable in gold unless it suited the Treasury, the option of funding them in interest-bearing notes being the alternative, and a date was fixed, generally three years from the date of the notes, before which redemption in any form could not be exacted.

In 1819 the Government tried the experiment, though in a very cautious manner, of lending on land through loan commissioners. Loans were not to exceed £200 currency on real estate supposed to be worth three times as much, repayable in three, six and nine years, with six per cent. per annum interest.

In 1826 the Government took a further downward step by providing that notes must be received by the public in payment of warrants on the Treasury, whenever the Treasury was not in possession of coin with which to make such payments. The next step, naturally, was to require the Treasury to retain all coin in order to make payments in connection with the funded debt, and this was soon followed by the requirement that the public must pay customs duties in coin. In 1834, the latter provision was somewhat ameliorated by permission to pay in Treasury notes—the pound in paper money being reckoned at sixteen shillings for customs payments. Various efforts at reform were made, and by 1846 customs duties were payable in coin and Treasury notes, but not in bank notes; and in order to aid in floating the Treasury issues, banks were not allowed to issue notes smaller than £5 currency ($20). The remaining evil features were not removed by the legislation of 1846, and practically continued until the redemption of the whole by the Dominion Government, beginning in 1867.

[redacted]

Returning to the province now called Quebec, it will be remembered that from 1815 to 1820 the army bill issues were being retired. The people had experienced the benefits of a well-regulated and elastic paper currency, but it was based upon the war requirements of the Government, and not upon the requirements of trade; these war requirements being at an end, trade must get along once more with the miscellaneous coinage of foreign countries, unless a basis for paper money issues could be found. The outcome of this fact was the Bank of Montreal, now possessing a capital and surplus of $18,000,000, and enjoying the distinction of being the most important monetary institution in North America. Without awaiting the consent of Parliament, articles of association were signed June 23, 1817, under which the capital was to be limited to £250,000 currency. In August, the Bank commenced business, and at the next session of the Legislature, an act incorporating it was passed, but was withheld by the Governor in order to obtain the royal assent. This was refused. In Quebec (city) another bank was founded on June 9, 1818, called the Quebec Bank, which is still doing a large business. Its capital was limited to £75,000 currency. It also began as a private bank, applied for incorporation in 1819, and, like the Bank of Montreal, failed to obtain it. A third bank, not now in existence, was established in Montreal in 1818, called the Bank of Canada, which also failed at this time to obtain incorporation. Its capital was limited to £200,000 currency.

During the session of 1820–21, however, the Legislature was again asked to grant charters to these three banks in conformity with their articles of association, and with such further regulations as Parliament might impose. The application was successful, and charters were granted by the Legislature in 1821, but did not receive the royal assent until 1822.

CHARTERS GRANTED TO THREE BANKS—THEIR PROVISIONS

As regards the development of banking, what we are most interested in at the present time is the nature of the charters granted to these three banks. They were all practically alike, and that granted to the Bank of Montreal may be taken as the type. It may safely be said that these first charters are the substructure on which all subsequent improvements have been built, and that no very radical changes have been at any time necessary. Indeed, there are very many provisions in these charters which were subsequently included, almost unchanged, in the general Banking Act. Among the provisions, which are not essentially different in principle from the present act, are the following:

1. The charter was to continue for ten years.

2. The directors were to be British subjects. The qualification in stockholding was quite small, viz., four shares of £50 currency each, or $800 par value. The directors were not to act as private bankers. They were to be remunerated only by compensation voted by shareholders at an annual meeting.

3. The directors were to appoint the officers of the bank and to take surety bonds for faithful performance of duties. They were to declare dividends, when profits were earned, as often as half-yearly. They must not, in paying dividends, encroach upon the capital. They must keep proper stock-books. They had the right to inspect all books, correspondence, and funds of the bank. They were obliged to submit a clear annual statement of the bank's position to the shareholders at the annual meeting.

4. The bank might receive deposits, deal in bills of exchange, discount notes, buy gold and silver coin and bullion, etc., but might not engage in business other than banking.

5. It could not lend money directly upon real property. It could, however, take such as further security for loans already made. It was not permitted to lend money to a foreign country.

6. It could issue notes to circulate as money, but with no limit other than the general limit for all obligations.

7. The Government might require at any time, for the protection of the public, a statement, under oath, of the position of the bank.

8. Transfers of shares in the bank were not valid unless registered in the stock-book of the bank, and the bank had a prior lien on the stock for ordinary debts due by the holder.

The following regulations, on the other hand, are different in principle from the general act now in force :

1. The total liabilities were not to exceed three times the capital stock actually paid in, and directors were personally liable if they permitted such excess. Any director might save himself by publicly protesting within eight days after the transactions causing the excess took place.

2. The shareholders were exempt from any liability except that of payment for the stock for which they had subscribed, with a penalty of five per cent. for non-payment after installments matured.

3. Voting by shareholders was not, as now, in exact proportion to shares held, the number of votes diminishing by a scale as the holdings increased ; so that while one share gave one vote, ten shares gave only five, and thirty shares only ten. No holding gave more than twenty votes.

The banks soon opened branches and agencies, and, imperfect in detail as it was at this time, the present system of banking began its career. From the first the banks exercised, under the scrutiny of Government and press, the great franchise of note issues unsecured by any special pledge ; they possessed the identity given by separate charters and clearly distinguishing titles ; they opened branches and assumed the widest functions of banking without discussing the precise powers accorded by these charters. Possessing capital quite as large relatively to the community as they have now, they assumed, without hesitation, a national position as clearing-houses for the exchange of the country's products.

BANKS FOUNDED IN UPPER CANADA

Leaving the province of Lower Canada (Quebec) and turning to Upper Canada (Ontario), we find that the people clearly saw the benefits of the paper issues of the War of 1812, and were strongly influenced by the growth of banking in Great Britain and the United States. In March, 1817, the House of Assembly was asked by the business men of Kingston to incorporate the Bank of Upper Canada ; so that the people of this province were not behind those of Lower Canada in seeking such privileges. The act was passed by the Provincial Parliament, but was reserved by the Lieutenant-Governor in order to obtain royal assent. This was not granted until April 21, 1821. Because of this delay the people of Kingston asked in June, 1819, for the incorporation of the Bank of Kingston, which was granted so far as the Provincial Parliament was concerned ; and the people of what is now Toronto, in July, 1819, asked for the incorporation of the Upper Canada Banking Company, which was granted but reserved for royal assent. The delay still continuing, the House of Assembly, on April 5, 1821, passed resolutions looking to the establishment of a Provincial Bank ; but the assent to the charter of the Bank of Upper Canada being proclaimed on the 21st of that month, no further action was necessary. In the nature of its charter, the Bank of Upper Canada did not differ materially from the banks of Lower Canada. Its capital was, after some discussion, settled, in 1823, at £100,000 currency, of which only a small proportion was actually paid in specie. Its head office was to be established at the seat of government, and the power to establish branches was directly stated. It became a semi-State institution by the fact that the Government subscribed for 2,000 shares (£12 10s. od. currency each), thus owning one-fourth of the stock, and was allowed to name four of the fifteen directors. The bank could buy real estate only for its own use, whereas in Lower Canada there was only a provision as to the annual value of real estate held by a bank. Inability to pay its notes in specie involved stoppage of business or forfeiture of charter until payments were resumed. The return to the Government was periodic instead of occasional, but was required only once a year. The charter extended to June 1, 1848.

In 1818, apparently, while awaiting a charter for the Bank of Upper Canada, the promoters in Kingston established a private bank under that name, as had been done by the originators of the Bank of Montreal and the Quebec Bank. When the charter was finally granted, the Provincial Government had subscribed for shares, and other changes had taken place, so that the chartered institution did not take over the business of the private bank, and the latter has, for this reason, been called the "pretended" Bank of Upper Canada. These two ventures are all, however, that resulted at the moment from the desire on the part of the people of Upper Canada for bank accommodation.

BANKS ESTABLISHED IN NOVA SCOTIA

Early in 1820, royal assent was given to a charter for the Bank of New Brunswick at St. John, with a capital of £50,000 currency. In Nova Scotia, although there had been, as we have said, agitation for a bank early in the century, the issue since 1812 of a Government currency acted as a deterrent, and it was not until 1825 that the Halifax Banking Company commenced business. It did so as a private bank, although since 1872 it has been a regularly chartered body, and it was not until 1832 that the first joint-stock bank, the Bank of Nova Scotia, was chartered. The capital of this bank was to be £100,000 currency, of which £50,000 was to be paid in in specie or Treasury notes before it commenced business. The important feature in which its charter varied from those granted in Lower and Upper Canada was in the introduction of the double liability of shareholders, or the liability in the event of failure, to pay assessments sufficient, after exhausting the ordinary assets, to meet all liabilities, provided such calls in the aggregate did not exceed the original amount of capital paid in. It was prohibited from issuing notes under 26 shillings, in order to preserve to the Government the exclusive issue of its notes for denominations from $5 downward.

We have now referred to three banks chartered in Lower Canada, one private and one chartered bank in Upper Canada, one chartered bank in New Brunswick, and one private and one chartered bank in Nova Scotia—in all, six chartered and two private banks. Of these several ventures, two, the Bank of Canada in Lower Canada, and the private or "pretended" Bank of Upper Canada, passed out of existence in a few years, so that banking in the various provinces now merged in the Dominion was practically inaugurated by the following institutions: The Bank of Montreal, the Quebec Bank, the Bank of Upper Canada, the Bank of New Brunswick, the Halifax Banking Company, and the Bank of Nova Scotia, and these are all successful institutions to-day except the Bank of Upper Canada, the failure of which in 1866, after a career of half a century, is the most serious calamity in the history of banking in Canada.

When we look at the map, the extent of country to be served by these six banks seems very great, but when we consider the population and the nature of the commerce, it is difficult to understand how they managed to survive. A scanty population settled here and there at seaside ports and on the shores of rivers and lakes, without means of communication worthy the name, without manufactures, with agriculture so little advanced that the products of the chase and the forest were still more important as exports than the results of farming, there was but little basis for sound banking, and its development lacked interest until many years after this period. In Lower Canada the volume of business considerably more than doubled, apparently, between 1820 and 1830, but in the latter year the figures, exclusive of the Bank of Canada, which was almost liquidated, were very trifling. The resources were as follows: Capital, £304,000; notes in circulation, £217,000; deposits, £163,000, while other items made the aggregate a little more than £700,000 currency. The assets to represent this were loans, £602,000, and cash, £103,000. In the same year a return of the one bank in Upper Canada shows resources as follows: Capital, £77,000; notes in circulation, £156,000; deposits and other debts due, £38,000, making an aggregate of less than £275,000 currency. This was represented by loans of £214,000, cash £23,000, and other assets of about £30,000.

GROWTH OF BANKING IN THE VARIOUS PROVINCES

We will now make a rapid survey of the growth of banking in the various provinces, pausing only to note the additions to the principles of banking, which were gradually being built up by experience. We have referred to the creation in 1820 of the Bank of New Brunswick; in that province the next charter was granted in 1825, to the Charlotte County Bank at St. Andrew's, with a capital of £15,000 currency. These charters were for twenty years, and the total liabilities were restricted to twice the paid-up capital, instead of three times, as in the other provinces. Otherwise they did not differ materially from those granted elsewhere. In 1834, the Central Bank of New Brunswick, at Fredericton, obtained a charter which contained the following conditions, resulting, apparently, from the recommendations of the Committee for Trade of His Majesty's Privy Council for 1830 and 1833:

1. No bank notes to be issued until one-half of the authorized capital stock was paid in (in the case of this bank this amounted to only £7,500 at first, the capital being but £15,000, but in 1836 the capital was increased to £50,000).

2. Public commissioners to count the cash in the vaults and ascertain that it was actual capital paid in.

3. The principle of double liability of stockholders, which had already been introduced in Nova Scotia.

4. Loans on pledge of Bank's own stock forbidden.

5. Liabilities of directors, directly or as sureties, limited to one-third of the paid-in capital

6. Semi-annual returns to the Government.

7. No bill offered for discount to be refused by vote of a single director—a very doubtful provision.

8. A director with debts in default to Bank not to attend board meetings.

While these were very considerable changes from the charters previously granted in New Brunswick, they did not materially advance the principles of banking, as most of these conditions already existed in one form or another in other provinces. In the same year, the Commercial Bank of New Brunswick, and in 1836 the St. Stephen's Bank, were created. In the charter of the latter it is provided that no stockholder should own more than twenty per cent. of the capital stock, and that the lien for a debt due the Bank upon shares in the Bank owned by the debtor shall not have priority to that of a creditor who seizes and sells under execution. The limitations as to proportion of the aggregate of debts to capital were materially altered by excluding deposits from the liabilities to be considered. In the same year authority was granted to the City Bank, with a head office at St. John, and a capital of £100,000, but it merged, in 1839, with the Bank of New Brunswick, which in 1837 had doubled its capital.

From this time until confederation, in 1867, the banking legislation of New Brunswick has little interest for us. Existing banks renewed their charters, accepting the new provisions, and sometimes increasing their capital; new banks were authorized, few of which actually began business. The result was that in 1867, when the province gave up its power to legislate regarding banking, there were in existence four banks, while there were five available charters not put in actual operation.

The history of banking in Nova Scotia prior to confederation is even more barren of incident than that of New Brunswick, but it is interesting because of the interference by Government in the business of banking in order to keep in circulation the Government issues already referred to, and the development of private banking, owing, doubtless, partly to the restrictions imposed by the Government in granting charters. Except that, in 1837 and 1838, the Bank of British North America, to be referred to hereafter, obtained permission to do business in New Brunswick and Nova Scotia, respectively, the latter province for many years depended for banking on the Bank of Nova Scotia and the private banks, and for currency on the issues of the Government, the Bank, and the private bankers. The private bankers were apparently only restricted in issuing notes by the condition that no note should be for less than £5 currency, which restriction was created by a statute of 1834 and also applied to the Bank of Nova Scotia. From 1841 to 1847, the charter of the Bank of Nova Scotia was several times extended for periods of one or two years at a time, and in 1847 it was renewed for ten years, the main addition being the penalty of loss of charter for an issue of bank notes causing the liabilities to exceed the legal limit of three times the paid-up capital. In 1856, it was again renewed for fifteen years and the authorized capital increased to £400,000 currency. Between this year and confederation, several charters were granted, but as they did not differ in principle from that of the Bank of Nova Scotia we need not refer further to them. At the time of confederation (1867) there were five banks doing business under charters from the province, and one charter not yet in use.

It will have been observed that there was during the period of provincial charters very little growth in banking principles in these two provinces, and it will not be necessary in a mere history of development to refer to them again.

NEW LEGISLATION RELATING TO NOTE ISSUES

In 1841, the provinces of Lower and Upper Canada (Quebec and Ontario) were united in the Province of Canada, but before considering the growth of banking under the legislation of that province, we must refer to facts of considerable importance which took place from about 1830 to 1841 in the two old provinces.

In Lower Canada, in 1830, an act was passed prohibiting, under forfeiture of the amount involved, the issue or use in payment of any note payable to bearer or for less than five dollars, except by a chartered bank. In renewing the charter of the Bank of Montreal in this year, which was only extended to 1837, there were also some interesting additional provisions. No notes were to be issued of less denomination than five shillings ($1), and the total of notes for smaller denominations than £1 5s. od. currency ($5), were not to exceed one-fifth of the capital stock. The Legislature might also at any time further restrict the issue of these small notes or suppress them entirely. The penalty for violating these two restrictions was forfeiture of charter. Improvements were made in the form of the return to Government, and in order that the province might not be left with a chartered institution enjoying the monopoly of banking, it was provided that in the event of the charter of the Quebec Bank not being renewed, the charter of the Bank of Montreal should also cease. These were somewhat illiberal provisions, and not very creditable to the legislators who imposed them. In 1831, the charter of the Quebec Bank was renewed until 1836, and later this was extended to the same day in 1837, on which that of the Bank of Montreal expired. The new provisions in the charter of the latter bank were also added, and it may be well to notice here that thus early there is the tendency to make all charters of banks expire at the same time—a feature, whether wise or not, which is very conspicuous in the present system.

Thus far, while the Bank of Montreal had a branch in Quebec, the Quebec Bank had no branch in Montreal, and in order to avoid monopoly, in 1831 a charter was asked for the City Bank. From the date of the founding of the original banks until Lower and Upper Canada merged in the Province of Canada, in 1841, this was the only proposal to establish a new chartered bank in Lower Canada, and yet it met with opposition, almost strong enough to defeat it, from the French members of the House of Assembly, whose naturally conservative instincts were still strongly averse to banks of issue. For reasons not material to our subject, royal assent was not granted until 1833, and the charter was to expire on the same day as those already granted—June 1, 1837. The conditions only differed from previous charters regarding the manner of paying in the capital, the two banks in existence having commenced as private ventures. The capital was to be £200,000 currency, and before commencing business must all be subscribed and £40,000 currency be paid up and actually in possession of the bank in current coin of the province. The whole capital must be paid within four years.

Owing to the Rebellion of 1837, there was created a body known as the "Special Council of the Province of Lower Canada," which, for the time being, governed the country. There was therefore no Parliament in 1837 to renew the three charters. The difficulty was got over by the Bank of Montreal continuing for a short time without incorporation and then having its charter extended for four years by this Special Council, while the other two banks secured royal letters patent, which continued their existence until one year after the next session of Parliament. The Quebec Bank subsequently obtained from the Special Council an express extension of its charter until 1842.

It will be remembered that private bankers, of whom there were doubtless many of one kind or another by this time, were forbidden to issue notes in Lower Canada intended for use as money. But the disorganized state of trade and finance, consequent upon the rebellion, had, notwithstanding the penalty, caused a flood of paper issues by private bankers and merchants, and the Special Council endeavored to improve the situation temporarily by granting licenses to issue such notes, for one year, to private bankers who complied with certain regulations. The issue of such illegitimate currency and the suspension of specie payments at this time, which will be referred to elsewhere, are, I believe, the only evidences which can be quoted of failure on the part of the bank note issuers, taken as a whole, to provide adequately for the currency requirements of the country, and these defects were entirely the result of the disorganization growing out of the rebellion.

BANKS WITH EXCEPTIONAL CHARTERS

We have next to refer to the creation of two institutions with charters possessing unusual features. When a general banking act was considered by the Dominion Government after confederation, these banks were the subject of various exemptions and requirements, because of the peculiar nature of the privileges they had already obtained. In 1835 a private banking firm was formed called Viger, DeWitt et Cie., also known as "La Banque du Peuple." It was simply a partnership of a kind frequently found in Europe. The twelve principal partners, who alone were to manage the business, were subject to the unlimited liability of ordinary partners in any firm, but they could have an indefinite number of special partners, or "commanditaires," whose liability ended with the payment of whatever shares in the venture they subscribed or accepted by transfer. This institution eventually became one of the chartered banks, but, as we have indicated, without losing its peculiar features. The "twelve principal partners" became practically the directors, retaining their unlimited liability, and the "commanditaires" became shareholders, without the double liability which inhered to stock held in other banks chartered by the Canadian Parliament. After a career of sixty years, this bank suspended in July, 1895, and having practically retired its note issues is, at the moment, endeavoring to arrange with its depositors to form a small bank of the ordinary character, thus removing from our system one of the few remaining anomalous features inherited from the legislation preceding confederation. In 1836 a bank was formed in England to do business through branches in the various North American provinces, a thing not done at the moment and which would require legislation in each of the provinces. Partly in order to avoid this, it secured a royal charter and thereafter obtained whatever local legislation was at the time necessary, and began business as the Bank of British North America, with a nominal capital of £1,000,000 sterling, which was eventually paid up in full, but without double liability of shareholders, and with power to issue no notes smaller than £1 currency.

BANKING PROGRESS IN UPPER CANADA

In Upper Canada we have to deal with very different conditions and a different people. At present the wealthiest of the provinces, it was at the time of the founding of the Bank of Upper Canada little more than a primæval forest, broken along the lakes and rivers by a few communities where the people struggled bravely for a livelihood, for the most part without the aid of roads or any public improvements. They were not, like their French-Canadian brothers, unwilling to try joint-stock banking; they were only too willing to try anything which promised to oil the wheels of trade. In this spirit they began in 1825 the building of that series of canals which aided so much in making the lakes continuously navigable, and while they had to wait many years for the realization of their schemes, the expenditure of so much money and the immigration which at this time flowed in from Great Britain gave a great impetus to the development of the province. As might be expected, it was the day of strong rather than of scrupulous men. The government was in the hands of a powerful clique bent on controlling the religion, education, and the settlement as well as the legislation of the country. With this body the Bank of Upper Canada was closely allied, and, whether justly or not, was accused of using its power in politics. Be this as it may, in 1830-31 a bill for the creation of a bank was rejected by the Legislative Council, which is said to have been controlled by this clique, and in 1833 two bills were also rejected after having been passed by the Assembly. But the paid-up capital of the Bank of Upper Canada, which in 1823 was only £10,640 currency, had been increased until in 1830 it had reached the limit of £100,000 currency. It had paid dividends at eight per cent. per annum and had twice paid bonuses of six per cent. While the Legislative Council refused charters to new corporations, this one bank was permitted in 1831-32 to increase its capital by another £100,000 currency. At the same time one of the bills referred to above as having been rejected was passed, creating the Commercial Bank of the Midland District, with its head office at Kingston and an authorized capital of £100,000 currency. The improvements in principle in the bills passed at this time, regarding the two banks, were not very important. They were forbidden to lend on their own stock on penalty of forfeiting their charters, and more elaborate returns to Government were required than hitherto. So ready were the people to aid in extending banking that the subscriptions for the £100,000 currency of new stock of the Bank of Upper Canada, the books being open for but one day and no subscription permitted for more than eighty shares (£12 10s. od. currency, or $50 each), amounted to £300,987 10s. od. currency. The premium received was sufficient to enable a bonus to be paid to original shareholders of eighteen per cent. in addition to the ordinary dividend of eight per cent.

We have already referred in dealing with New Brunswick to certain recommendations of the Committee for Trade of the Privy Council made as early as 1830, regarding colonial bank charters. These had not been considered in the recent bank legislation of Upper Canada, and there was in consequence a threat of royal disallowance unless the proposed conditions were added. But the banks had acted for a year under the new legislation and had already as many as fifteen or sixteen branches or agencies, with discounts amounting to £450,000 currency and notes in circulation of about £300,000 currency, so that the mere possibility of disallowance caused financial trouble. The people protested and petitioned the King, and in the end a compromise was reached. The recommendations, mostly excellent in themselves, were in substance as follows:

1. Bank charters to be forfeited by suspension for sixty days consecutively, or during a year.

2. Note issues to be dated where issued and to be redeemed in specie there and at head office. No branch need redeem notes issued at another branch or at head office.

3. One-half of capital to be paid in at commencement, the remainder at discretion.

4. The directors not to become liable on obligations to bank exceeding one-third of the total discounts of bank.

5. Bank not to hold its own stock or lend money thereon.

6. Half-yearly statements to Government of average assets and liabilities made from weekly balance-sheets, with particulars of dividends and reserved profits. Special returns might be called for and must be verified under oath if required.

7. Shareholders subject to double liability.

8. Banks not to lend on real estate.

These were referred to a special committee of the Upper Canada House of Assembly, who heard bankers and merchants in evidence and eventually reported strongly against the interference, particularly against the 1st, 2nd and 6th of the recommendations. On the 7th they did not agree, and the 8th was already incorporated in existing charters, while the 3rd, 4th and 5th were admitted in principle and acted upon. With the concurrence of the new Commercial Bank, a bill was reported adding to its charter the 3rd, 4th, 5th and 7th provisions, but at the same time an address to the King was prepared deploring the royal veto and praying that the new provisions be not required. As the address passed by a vote of thirty-one to one, action was delayed on the bill amending the Commercial Bank charter, and in consequence of the feeling aroused, the original legislation was not disallowed. What is noticeable at this time is not the rejection by the

Upper Canadians of recommendations good enough in themselves, but their intelligent appreciation of the value of banks and their determination to manage their own affairs.

In 1835, the Gore Bank was incorporated, with its head office at Hamilton, and an authorized capital of £100,000 currency. In its charter the 2nd, 5th, 7th and 8th of the recommendations were included, and royal assent was promptly given. In the same year the Commercial Bank increased its authorized capital from £100,000 currency to £200,000 currency, and the 4th and 5th recommendations were added to its charter, the 8th already being included. The others were not included, yet the legislation was not disallowed.

These evidences of growth do not represent fully the desires of the people at this time, but rather the meagre extent to which a powerfully intrenched government chose to meet the public demands. The opposition apparently clamored for legislation to make banking "free." In 1831, 1831-32, 1833-34, 1835 and 1836, measures were proposed looking toward uniformity in the system of banking and freedom to all to engage in the business who should conform to the proposed laws. But it was still quite easy to establish a private bank which might issue notes, no act prohibiting private issues being yet in force in Upper Canada. Aided by this fact, in 1835 some politicians opposed to the present banking system organized, by a deed of settlement, a private bank known as the Farmers' Joint Stock Banking Company, with a capital not larger than £50,000 currency; and later, in the same year, the Bank of the People, which, in the course of a year, got together a capital of about £13,000 currency, began business. At the same time some Americans opened the Niagara Suspension Bridge Bank, with an agency at Lockport, N.Y., and one in Canada, at Chippewa, and with even less capital than the last-named concern. Messrs. Truscott & Green also began business as the Agricultural Bank. Very naturally, this brought forward for prompt consideration the question of private note issues, and in 1837 legislation was obtained prohibiting the issue without legislative authority of notes intended to pass as money. It was found expedient, however, to make an exception in favor of the four private banks above referred to.

PUBLIC CLAMOR FOR MORE BANKS—RESTRAINT FROM THE COLONIAL OFFICE

The people of the province were in many ways contributing towards the creation of the commercial panic of 1837, which left its mark for many years on the trade of North America. They were speculating in land, making public improvements on an ambitious scale, attempting to manufacture a few articles, and trading generally much beyond their financial capacity. They were, therefore, in the state of mind which has so often characterized American communities when deeply in debt—they wanted banks, because they thought that the creation of such institutions would make it easier to borrow, and they wanted paper money, of any sort, for equally unsound reasons. During the ten years preceding the union of Lower and Upper Canada, in 1841, there were about twenty-five public bills in Upper Canada on the subject of banking and currency which did not pass, while in 1833 the Assembly did pass a bill authorizing the Receiver-General to issue currency, and in 1835 a committee reported favorably on a plan for a provincial bank, which was to issue notes based on the public debt and use its profits to pay the interest on the same. Fortunately, these schemes did not become law. In 1836-37, bills were passed which, if assented to, would have increased the banking capital from £500,000 currency to £4,590,000 currency, and have added nine new banks to the number doing business in a province which contained only about 400,000 people. The province did not as yet enjoy the benefits of home rule, and consequently resisted bitterly all interference on the part of the Colonial Office in England, but every intelligent Canadian must now see quite clearly that had we been allowed our own way in banking and currency legislation at this time, we should doubtless have tried, one after the other, the entire round of unsound experiments, and would to-day be perhaps not very anxious to discuss the soundness of our banking system. When bills were passed in the various provinces they were given the force of law by the Lieutenant-Governor, without waiting to ascertain whether or not they were to meet the fate of royal disallowance, and, consequently, contracts having been entered into on the faith of the legislation, it was found impracticable, or at all events unwise, to insist on disallowance. To avoid this difficulty the Colonial Office, in 1836, succeeded in having instructions sent out to the Lieutenant-Governor not to permit legislation bearing upon any kind of notes intended to pass as money to go into effect without first receiving the royal assent. The House of Assembly, of course, resisted, and the home authorities were very conscious of the danger of interference; but any student of joint-stock banking in England will understand how honestly alarmed the British authorities must have been at the wild pace of joint-stock banking throughout North America at this time. The Colonial Office therefore persisted in demanding a reference of such measures for royal allowance before legislation was put in force, and as a result, the extraordinary acts of 1836-37 were not allowed, but were referred back for further consideration by the Upper Canadian authorities. None of the bills were again approved in Canada, the period of inflation having passed its meridian. The Government of Upper Canada having refused to be guided by the series of recommendations by the Committee for Trade (of which an abstract has already been given), and being deeply irritated by the instructions to refer all currency measures for royal allowance before putting such legislation in force, the Secretary of State for the Colonies forwarded a second series of recommendations by the Committee for Trade, upon the observance of which by the Canadian Parliament reference for royal assent in advance of action upon legislation became no longer necessary.

UNSOUND BANKING

There is little to be learned by a study of the kind of business transacted by the banks of Upper Canada at this time. In the nature of things, it was not very sound banking. The people were chiefly concerned in actually clearing up the forest or in improving the first rude conditions of settlement. Therefore, the results were apt to show mainly in connection with real property, and there were not only too many loans asked and granted where there was no intention of creating or moving merchantable products with the money, but there must have been a constant tendency for loans made on the basis of creating or moving merchantable products to drift into loans resting on real property. Still the fact remains that there had not been, nor was there destined to be for many years to come, a failure of a joint-stock bank in this province. The system was in many respects bad, but there must have been more good than bad in an actual practice of banking which, for the first forty years of its history, escaped the disgrace of failure. That this was partly due to the high credit enjoyed by the few joint-stock institutions, especially when compared with the private concerns, there is little doubt. The volume of business in 1837 was as follows: Capital stock paid up of the three chartered banks, £476,978; of the four private banks, £98,023; notes in circulation respectively, £319,244 and £71,148; deposits, £204,571 and £12,328; specie, £78,884 and £14,457; loans and discounts, £895,039 and £143,718. If we multiply the paid-up capital of the three chartered banks by three, we find the aggregate of their permissible liabilities to be £1,430,934, and as their deposits amounted to only £204,571, there was left the sum of £1,226,363 to cover debts due to foreign correspondents and notes in circulation. Their debts to foreign correspondents, if any, were inconsiderable, and, therefore, while they had legal power to circulate notes to the extent of £1,000,000 to £1,250,000 currency, they had notes outstanding for only £319,244. In 1826 the Bank of Upper Canada was able to keep out notes to the extent of two and a half times its capital; by 1831 this had fallen to one and seven-eighths, and by 1837, because of the competition of other banks, and doubtless also because of better means of communication, all of the banks circulated much less than the amount of paid-up capital. None of the banks issued notes payable at any point except at the head office, but there were seven branches in existence performing the same functions as branches do now, while there were agencies with limited functions numbering at least twelve, and probably several more. These were all connected with the Bank of Upper Canada and the Commercial Bank, the Gore Bank having as yet opened no branches or agencies.

THE PANIC OF 1837

This was the condition of banking in Upper Canada when it was called upon, in common with Lower Canada, to meet the financial troubles arising from the rebellion at home and the business panic in the United States in 1837. Early in May, 1837, there was a general suspension of specie payments in the United States, and, within a week, the banks in Lower Canada also suspended payments in specie. There had been a great expansion of credit throughout North America, and now that the inevitable contraction had set in, gold was required for export. Canada already made a large proportion of its sterling purchases and other money settlements in New York, and was at once affected by the collapse of credit and consequent suspension of payments in exportable money. But in Upper Canada, whether from ignorance, sentiment, or intelligent courage, the banks continued to redeem. By the middle of June the circulation of the three chartered and four private banks had fallen from £508,896 on May 15th, to £390,392, while in the same month the specie fell from £120,789 to £93,341, although the Bank of Upper Canada had imported £40,000. At this time, the public, suffering from two bad harvests, unable to obtain any discounts from the banks, or advances on products shipped to Lower Canada, were in a bad way; and to add to their troubles, the fiscal agents in England of the province failed. On the 19th of June a special meeting of the Legislature was held because of the financial situation. Sir Francis Bond Head, the Lieutenant-Governor, urged that the banks pay in specie until forced to stop. He begged them not to yield to what he believed to be dishonorable and a breach of contract. But the Legislature, by the 11th of July, passed a measure of relief for the entire seven banks, chartered and private. On procuring from the

Governor-in-Council an order of authority, a bank was relieved from the necessity of closing its doors on refusing to redeem its notes. The bank might be forced to expose fully to Government the state of its affairs, and special conditions might be imposed in the discretion of the Lieutenant-Governor. The suspension might last until the end of the next session of Parliament, and during this period banks were not to issue notes beyond the amount of paid-up capital, and were to use all specie in their possession for purposes of redemption excepting only what might be necessary for change-making purposes.

SUSPENSION OF BANKS AND POPULAR REBELLION

But the banks did not hasten to take advantage of the offered relief, and it is evident that they intended to pull through, if at all possible, without discredit. In September, however, the Commercial Bank took advantage of the act and was permitted to suspend payments in specie. In November, the private bank of Truscott, Green & Co., known as the Agricultural Bank, failed, the partners leaving the country. Later in the year, the Farmers' Bank suspended for about two months. The Bank of Upper Canada and the Gore Bank still continued to pay, although the notes of the former in circulation fell from £212,000 in May to £80,000 in December. Apparently, they were now anxious to suspend, but the Lieutenant-Governor was obstinate regarding the Bank of Upper Canada, claiming that it was, in a sense, a Government bank, and the Gore Bank desired to act in harmony with its more important neighbor in that part of Upper Canada. In November there was actual armed rebellion in Lower Canada, which, however, was put down by the middle of December. Early in December there was similar trouble in Upper Canada, which lasted only a few days. This was followed by an invasion by Americans, also of small proportions, but sufficient to cause the Government to require large advances from the Bank of Upper Canada. The Bank stood up for a time against the strain, but early in March, 1838, it received permission to suspend specie payments, in which it was immediately followed by the Gore Bank. At the same time an act was passed extending the limit of note issues to twice the paid-up capital and permitting the disposal of specie for other purposes than the redemption of notes.

RESUMPTION OF PAYMENTS

By June, 1838, the banks in the United States and in Lower Canada, generally, resumed specie payments, but the Bank of Upper Canada objected to such an early resumption in the province of Upper Canada. By November there was another rebellion in Lower Canada, necessitating another suspension there. After much discussion resumption was effected in Lower Canada in June, 1839, and in Upper Canada in November of that year. During the periods of suspension there was evidently considerable practical redemption by the sale of bills of exchange on England, although the rate charged amounted to redemption at a discount of one to two per cent. and for some months at three to eight per cent., and while discounts were by some banks much restricted, the business interests of the country were at no time actually paralyzed, and the banks continued to earn handsome dividends. Nevertheless, all the usual facts concurrent with rebellion and panic had to be borne, such as a general decline in exports, a fall in prices, stoppage of immigration, etc.

During 1838, the Bank of Montreal, at this time legally incapable of doing business in the province of Upper Canada, purchased the private bank known as the Bank of the People, and thus began the enormous business now done by the former bank in the province now called Ontario.

The Government was not altogether free from the desire to issue paper currency during this trying period, but, owing to the determination of the home authorities, such proposals failed to obtain royal assent and no such issues were made. The Government was obliged during this period to borrow on its stock in the Bank of Upper Canada, and in 1840 the Receiver-General was authorized to sell the stock, thus ending the connection of the Government with the Bank so far as holding stock is concerned. In February, 1841, the provinces of Lower and Upper Canada were united in the "Province of Canada."

CHAPTER III

1841-1867

BANKING IN OLD CANADA

STEPS TOWARD UNIFORM REGULATION OF BANKING

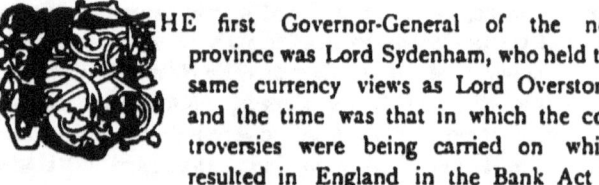

THE first Governor-General of the new province was Lord Sydenham, who held the same currency views as Lord Overstone, and the time was that in which the controversies were being carried on which resulted in England in the Bank Act of 1844. Lord Sydenham favored for Canada a provincial bank of issue, and he outlined a scheme under which he proposed to cancel the right of issue by the chartered banks, remunerating them therefor; and by giving it to this institution, which was not to do a general banking business, he hoped to make a large profit for the Government. He proposed a gold reserve of one-fourth of the issue, to which a maximum was fixed, with Government bonds for the balance, and he claimed that such a system would ensure ready convertibility. But the Canadian people were intelligent enough to see the defects of such a system, and, apart from other faults, the lack of elasticity alone condemned it. It was opposed, of course, by the banks, but also on many grounds by the general public, and did not become law. The Legislature, however, took advantage of the opportunity to impose a tax on bank notes of one per cent. per annum on the average in circulation.

The union of the two provinces emphasized the importance of uniformity in banking, and a committee on banking and currency, after considering the recommendations of the Home Government, contained in the dispatch of Lord Russell of

May 4, 1840, already referred to, reported in favor of the following restrictions:

1st. The amount of capital of the company to be fixed; and the whole of such fixed amount to be subscribed for within a limited period, not exceeding eighteen months from the date of the charter or Act of Incorporation.

2nd. The bank not to commence business until the whole of the capital is subscribed, and a moiety at least of the subscription paid up.

3rd. The amount of the capital to be paid up within a given time from the date of the charter or Act of Incorporation, such period, unless under particular circumstances, not to exceed two years.

4th. The debts and engagements of the company, on promissory notes or otherwise, not to exceed at any time thrice the amount of the paid-up capital, with the addition of the amount of such deposits as may be made with the company's establishment by individuals in specie or Government paper.

5th. All promissory notes of the company, whether issued from the principal establishment or from the branch banks, are to bear date at the place of issue, and to be payable on demand in specie at the place of date.

6th. Suspension of specie payments on demand at any of the company's establishments, for a given number of days (not in any case exceeding sixty) within any one year, either consecutively or at intervals, to forfeit the charter.

7th. The company shall not hold shares in its own stock, nor make advances on the security of their own shares.

8th. The company shall not advance money on security of lands, or houses, or ships, or on pledge of merchandise, nor hold lands or houses, except for the transaction of its business; nor own ships or be engaged in trade, except as dealers in bullion or bills of exchange; but shall confine its transactions to discounting commercial paper and negotiable securities and other legitimate banking business.

9th. The dividends to shareholders are to be made out of profits only, and not out of the capital of the company.

10th. The company to make up and publish periodical statements of its assets and liabilities (half-yearly or yearly), showing, under the heads specified in the annexed form, the average of the amount of its notes in circulation, and other liabilities at the termination of each week or month, during the period to which the statement refers, and the average amount of specie or other assets that were available to meet the same. Copies of these statements are to be submitted to the Provincial Government, and the company be prepared, if called upon, to verify such statements, by the production, as confidential documents, of the weekly or monthly balance sheets from which the same are compiled. And also to be prepared upon requisition from the Lords Commissioners of Her Majesty's Treasury, to furnish in like manner such further information respecting the state or proceedings of its banking establishments as their Lordships may see fit to call for.

11th. No by-law of the company shall be repugnant to the conditions of the charter or Act of Incorporation, or the statutes of the province.

12th. As the insertion in charters or Acts of Incorporation of provisions relating to the detailed management of the business of the corporation has, in several instances, been found to render the documents complicated and unintelligible, and has been productive of great inconvenience, it is desirable that such insertion should be avoided, and that the provisions of such charters or Acts of Incorporation should be confined, as far as practicable, to the special powers and privileges to be conferred on the company, and the conditions to be observed by the company, and to such general regulations relating to the nomination and powers of the directors, the institution of by-laws, or other proceedings of the company, as may be necessary, with a view to public convenience and security.

13th. No company to be allowed to issue its promissory notes payable on demand, to an amount greater than its paid-up capital.

FORM OF RETURN REFERRED TO IN REGULATION 10

Return of the average amount of Liabilities and Assets of the Bank of——during the period from (1st January) to (30th June) 184—.

Promissory notes in circulation not bearing interest	£——
Bills of exchange in circulation not bearing interest	£——
Bills and notes in circulation bearing interest	£——
Balances due to other banks	£——
Cash deposits not bearing interest	£——
" " bearing interest	£——
Total average liabilities	£——
Coin and bullion	£——
Landed or other property of the corporation	£——
Government securities	£——
Promissory notes or bills of other banks	£——
Balances due from other banks	£——
Notes and bills discounted or other debts due to the corporation not included under the foregoing heads	£——
Total average assets	£——

In the renewal by the new province of Canada of the charters granted by the old provinces of Lower and Upper Canada, these restrictions, in addition to most of the provisions to protect the public already mentioned, were observed, and thus the provision for the double liability of shareholders in the event of failure was imposed for the first time on the banks of Lower Canada.

Once more, by a dispatch dated 30th May, 1846, the home authorities furnished "Revised Regulations to be Observed in Incorporating Banking Companies in the Colonies." In this dispatch, after ineffectually urging, as in 1840, the abolition of the notes of smaller denominations than £1, twenty new regulations were proposed. Although eventually the banking system conformed to most of these regulations, they were not of sufficient importance to be noticed here.

We have now ascertained the principles at the base of banking in the old province of Canada, and which eventually made the foundation of the banking legislation of the confederation of the British North American provinces brought about in 1867. There were, however, two aberrations from sound principles to which I must refer, one of which was of short duration, while the other still exists as the one serious blot on our currency system.

"FREE BANKING ACT OF 1850"

The first of these aberrations was the so-called "Free Banking Act of 1850." Anyone having the opportunity to examine the correspondence of a Canadian bank at this time would at once realize how close were the trading and financial relations of Upper Canada and New York State, relations relatively much more important than now. The leading bankers of many of the large cities of the State were well-known individually to leading bankers in Upper Canada, and, apart from the mere routine of business, an extensive correspondence was carried on. In Canada, the experiment was being tried of banks specially chartered, with large capital, and branches, and with a circulation not specially secured. The banks had come through the trying times of 1847-48 without suspension or failure, but they did not open branches fast enough to satisfy the most enterprising of the business community; the Provincial Government was straitened financially, and the people had the common delusion that there was not enough money in circulation. In New York State, the opposite policy of banks with small capital, no branches, and a specially secured circulation was on trial; but the people of that State were so much more prosperous than the people of Canada, that it is not strange that many desired to try the banking system which had apparently contributed toward such good results. In consequence, a measure was passed entitled "An Act to Establish Freedom of Banking in this Province, etc.," having for its object the creation, under a general act and not by special charter, of small banks without branches, with a circulation based upon the securities of the province. It was hoped that this would have the effect of creating a market for such securitie[illegible]n privileges as still existed under which in lower Canada private bankers might issue notes were repealed, and any existing chartered bank might, in part or as a whole, surrender circulation under the unsecured system and issue under the secured system, thus escaping the tax of one per cent. per annum from which the secured notes were exempt. Indeed, by subsequent amendments stronger inducements were offered. Of the chartered banks, the Bank of British North America alone made use of the new act, and only because of a special disability under which it labored. Being established by royal charter, and the British authorities having been at all times opposed to notes of smaller denominations than £1 currency ($4), it had not, in common with the other banks whose charters were Canadian in origin, the right to issue notes of as low a denomination as five shillings currency ($1). It was accordingly benefited by taking advantage of the new act to the extent of the notes of small denominations required in its business. Altogether, only five banks with these limited privileges came into existence under this act. The minimum capital required was £25,000 currency ($100,000), and at the highest point the circulation in notes of small denominations by the Bank of British North America was greater than the entire circulation of the five free banks, while the total was only a little over £300,000 currency. In ten years, the system had practically come to an end, the only bank continuing to issue notes being the Bank of British North America, which, because of the disability already mentioned, issued its small notes under the free banking act until 1870, when the Dominion Government took from all banks the right to issue notes of less denomination than $4, and subsequently all smaller than $5, reserving the privilege for its own issues. Of the five banks thus created, two retired their notes and other obligations and went out of business, and three obtained charters, and were thus enabled to issue notes not specially secured. No attempt is here made to explain in detail the free banking system, because in Canada it left practically no enduring result of its former existence, and the reader can study it to better advantage in its origin and development in the United States. A very full account of the Canadian experiment will be found, however, in the first volume, page 154, of the "Journal of the Canadian Bankers' Association, 1893-94."

INCREASE OF BANK CAPITAL AUTHORIZED

Although the free banking experiment did not actually end until some years later, its failure, as early as 1854, was clearly apparent and the demand for increased banking capital had not been satisfied. The Legislature, therefore, relaxing somewhat the conditions hitherto imposed, granted permission to six existing banks to increase capital in the aggregate to the extent of about £2,000,000 currency, requiring them, however, to invest one-tenth of the paid-up capital in securities of the province. From this time there has, indeed, always been a disposition, although not to a serious extent, to make the banks, in exchange for their franchise, carry a portion of the public debt. In the same year the treaty for reciprocal relations in trade between Canada and the United States was passed, and the great impetus given thereby to business was naturally accompanied by the granting of several new bank charters. From 1855 to 1866, inclusive, more than twenty-five charters were granted, including the three free banks, which had decided to come under the ordinary system, and of these about fifteen banks actually came into existence. Two or three of them failed or were wound up voluntarily within a few years, and one was absorbed by amalgamation, but the remaining institutions, with two exceptions, are in existence at the present time.

The few years preceding 1857 had been in Canada as elsewhere years of great expansion in trade, while the building of Government-aided railroads and speculation in real estate were carried on at a pace of feverish excitement hitherto unknown in this country of moderate development. The Bank of Upper Canada was still the leading bank in that western portion of the province of Canada which before the Union had been known as Upper Canada. Down to 1857 it had paid large dividends and had apparently enjoyed great prosperity. Through the financial trouble of 1857 the Canadian banks were successful in preserving the strong credit which had always characterized them—they did not suspend specie payments—but the seeds had been sown for trouble of a more momentous nature than any previous experience, or any which Canadian banks have been called upon to suffer since that period. The area served by the Bank of Upper Canada and its branches was the most daring in its enterprise of any portion of Canada. There the railroad-building assumed greatest proportions and land speculation reached its craziest extremes. The Bank of Upper Canada had too freely aided new enterprises and had built up a capital of over $3,000,000,* on which even in 1858 it paid a dividend of eight per cent. By 1861 some of its errors had been realized and there was a change of administration in the Bank, in consequence of which the capital was cut down to $1,900,000. At this time the business of the Government, which it had for many years enjoyed, was transferred to the Bank of Montreal. After these events the Bank of Upper Canada enjoyed still a large measure of respect because of its past history, but maintained only a waning existence. In 1866 it failed. The failure was not

*In 1857 the decimal currency was adopted in Canada, and hereafter sums of Canadian money are expressed in dollars.

only disastrous, but the winding up of the bank was involved to a certain extent in mystery. The Government, for reasons not very apparent, did not press the collection of the double liability from the shareholders and paid off creditors at seventy-five cents on the dollar, losing, it is believed, all of its own claim of over a million of dollars. But, although the winding up of the Bank was conducted in a manner which would be impossible now, the rude shock to the confidence of the public in banks was sufficiently effective; and this first great disaster was not an unmixed evil.

A GOVERNMENT BANK OF ISSUE PROPOSED

We now come to the second aberration from the path of virtue in finance to which reference has been made. In 1859, the Minister of Finance, professing concern regarding the security for bank note issues and the general conduct of banking, but perhaps having quite as much in mind his own difficulties in carrying on provincial finances, instituted an inquiry through a committee on banking and currency, and followed this up by proposing in 1860 the establishment of a provincial bank of issue not unlike that proposed by Lord Sydenham. The issue by the Government of legal-tender notes would create a currency the prompt payment of which on demand, it was pretended, would be more assured than if issued by the banks. He was, however, unsuccessful, his proposal not being acceptable to the Legislature. But in 1866 the needs of the province were of such a nature that a somewhat similar proposal was brought forward, and this time with at least partial success. The Minister did not dare to press strongly for the entire separation of note-issuing from the other functions of banking and the assumption of this particular function by the Government through a mere bank of issue, because it was evident the people were not prepared for such a change. The Government had a floating debt, however, of about $5,000,000, nearly half of which was owed to its Canadian banker, the Bank of Montreal. The balance, doubtless, was largely due in England and might have to be provided from Canada. Its debentures were at a discount of about fifteen per cent. and it could not afford to consider the principles of finance too closely. The Minister, in language often heard before and since, talked of resuming some of the privileges hitherto deputed to others and of paying the debts of the country with the currency which it had the right to issue, etc., but the condition of the provincial finances was the strongest argument. As a result, power was obtained to issue notes payable in specie at Montreal and Toronto which should be a legal tender. The amount was to be fixed from time to time by authority of the Governor-in-Council, but the maximum was not to exceed $8,000,000.

Instead of directly forcing the banks to retire their notes in circulation, inducements were offered to cover the period until their charters expired, the intention being to take away the privilege when charters were renewed. To any bank voluntarily resigning its right to circulate notes, the Government offered to pay five per cent. per annum on the amount of its notes outstanding on April 30, 1866, until the date of the expiry of its charter, and the bank was to be allowed until January 1, 1868, to complete the withdrawal of its notes. For the issue and redemption of the Government notes which these banks would use in place of their own, the Government agreed to pay one-quarter of one per cent. every three months on the average amount kept in circulation. Finally, banks giving up their privilege of circulating notes were to be relieved from the requirement, already referred to, of investing ten per cent. of their capital in provincial bonds, and were at liberty to exchange them for the new provincial notes. The reserve to be held by the Government for its outstanding note issues was as follows: Until the issues exceeded $5,000,000, twenty per cent. in specie, and the balance in bonds of the province. For circulation in excess of $5,000,000, the specie reserve to be twenty-five per cent., with a corresponding reduction in the provincial bonds held for the remainder.

The total circulation of all Canadian banks at this time was about $10,000,000, of which the Bank of Montreal enjoyed over thirty per cent. As we have already stated, the Government was in debt to the Bank for over $2,000,000 at this time, and the bank was by law required to hold ten per cent. of its capital in provincial bonds, so that it must have owned at least $600,000 in these bonds, its capital being at this time $6,000,000. Had it been practicable for the remaining Canadian banks, and had they been willing, to retire their circulation and accept the commuted profit, the effect upon the finances and trade of the country of the withdrawal of so much capital could only have been general bankruptcy. But the Bank of Montreal was in a position to retire its circulation without disturbing its advances to the public, inasmuch as it would receive from the Government in exchange for the debt due the Bank, and for the provincial bonds it held, an amount of the new provincial currency in excess of any possible contraction of its own issues for some years to come. It therefore readily accepted the new conditions, while the other banks did not. The Bank of Montreal, already the bankers and now the note-issuing agency of the Government, was thus almost placed in the position of a State bank, and, rightly or wrongly, there was apparently a division of interest between it and the other banks which led to unfortunate results. The country was again experiencing a period of inflation, the circulation of the banks, in consequence, rapidly expanding; and it must have been a source of irritation to the Government and the Bank of Montreal that the aggregate of circulation in 1867 by the remaining banks was about $1,700,000 higher than in 1866, while that of the Government in actual circulation, added to such notes of the Bank of Montreal as were yet unredeemed, made a total considerably less than the circulation of the Bank of Montreal before the change. On the other hand, the banks circulating their own notes were at a disadvantage at the various points where settlements had to be made with the Bank of Montreal. The former would generally be the debtors, because of the volume of their notes falling into the hands of the Bank of Montreal, and not offset by similar notes of that bank coming into their hands. The Bank of Montreal could demand payment in gold or in the new legal tenders instead of the ordinary method of settlement by draft on some commercial centre. To get over this difficulty the various banks appear to have agreed with the Bank of Montreal to hold at the minimum a certain amount of the new legal tenders, the aggregate of the minima of all the banks being $1,000,000.

To add to other causes of irritation between the Bank of Montreal and its weaker brethren, a financial panic was brought about by the suspension of one of the most important banks in the western part of Canada, caused by large advances to a railroad company. The bank eventually was amalgamated with another, the shareholders saving a portion of their investment; but, owing to differences of interest and opinion between the Bank of Montreal and the others as to the assistance to be rendered to the institution in trouble, delay and doubt caused runs upon other western banks. The bank which suspended had a capital of $4,000,000, and being undoubtedly solvent, should not have been allowed to suspend if it had been at all possible, by harmonious action, to have liquidated its debts with open doors. The failure of the Bank of Upper Canada had caused the public to be extremely sensitive, and had there been unanimity of interest, the suspension of a second large bank, followed by a panic regarding other institutions, would doubtless have been averted.

Without entering into the question of the extent to which the unsound legislation contained in the Provincial Note Act contributed to the disasters of 1867, its passage certainly darkened the general cloud which hung over the history of Canadian finances at this moment. On July 1, 1867, a few months before the suspension of the bank which caused the panic, the Provincial Government of Canada came to an end, merging into that of the present Dominion of Canada.

NOTE.—The history of joint-stock banking in the provinces previous to confederation, contained in chapters 2 and 3, has been compressed as much as possible, not only because the space at the command of the writer is limited, but because the present sketch purports to be a history of development and principles rather than of the incidents of Canadian banking. In the chapter to follow, the writer deals with what has happened in his own time and experience, but for the facts dealt with in chapters 2 and 3 he is almost entirely indebted to the very comprehensive history by Dr. Breckenridge, entitled "The Canadian Banking System," and published in the second volume of the "Journal of the Canadian Bankers' Association, 1894-95." The reader who desires ampler information is referred to that excellent work.

CHAPTER IV

BANKING UNDER THE DOMINION

THE PRESENT ACT

IN 1867, the Parliament of Great Britain, by a measure known as the British North America Act, empowered the various political divisions of British North America, or such of them as chose to do so, to confederate under the title of the Dominion of Canada. The province of Canada, which had been formed out of the older provinces of Lower and Upper Canada, was again divided into the present provinces of Quebec (Lower Canada) and Ontario (Upper Canada), and to these the maritime provinces of Nova Scotia and New Brunswick were added. Additions were rapidly made until the Dominion was formed as it now exists. It comprises the provinces of Quebec, Ontario, Nova Scotia, New Brunswick, Prince Edward Island, Manitoba and British Columbia, and the Northwest Territories, which are divided into five districts.

Under the British North America Act, the Federal Government (the Government of the Dominion as distinguished from those of the various provinces) alone possesses the power of legislating as to coinage, currency and banking. The situation as to banking which had to be considered by the new government, although rendered serious by the bank failures, was not very complicated. The two maritime provinces were not in their financial ideas very materially out of harmony with old Canada, and instead of being called upon to uproot the pernicious legal-tender system of Nova Scotia, the Dominion Government was, because of the recent act of old Canada, only too likely to continue the policy of borrowing money in such an easy manner. The banking acts passed in 1867, 1868 and 1869 need not detain us. They were in the main merely measures to continue under the authority of the Dominion and extend to its larger area the powers already enjoyed, harmonizing a few inconsistencies, extending until 1870 any charters which were at the point of expiry, and adopting on behalf of the Dominion the terms, with little alteration, of the Provincial Note Act. But although the author of the Provincial Note Act had found it necessary to resign because of its unpopularity and what was deemed to be his share in the bank failures, his successor was evidently possessed with the same mania. Early in 1868, he proposed to the House of Commons the creation of a Committee on Banking and Currency, and he, evidently with the aid of the Government's bankers, strove hard to create a public opinion in favor of a system not essentially different from the old free banking system and its powerful and at that time apparently successful offspring, the National Banking System of the United States. The Committee on Banking and Currency obtained evidence from a large number of bankers and business men, the most valuable result being the recommendations made by them for the improvement of the then existing system, and not the evidence for or against the proposed scheme. And although the Minister of Finance offered his measure in Parliament, the opposition was of such a character that it was not thought expedient to press the matter at that time. Within a few months the new Minister of Finance also resigned.

The task of framing a general bank act for the Dominion now fell to a Minister who, although he had strong predilections in favor of the English Bank Act of 1844, was wise enough to realize that the practical bankers of the country, in their desire to curb their own weaker members, if for no other reason, were probably the best guides as to the wisest course to be followed. Conferences were held with them, and in the Minister's remarks in introducing and debating the measure which he finally proposed, he admitted the inexpediency of adopting either the United States National Banking System or the older idea of a Government bank of issue; and in doing so he also admitted that the system of note issues not specially secured must be continued. But the act for the issuance of Government notes through banks, whose profits on their own issues, thus relinquished, had been replaced by a sum paid periodically by the Government in commutation thereof, created a difficulty which must first be disposed of. The Government's bankers had alone been willing to enter into this arrangement, and it was therefore now terminated by a compromise. The banks were thereafter prohibited from issuing notes smaller than $4 (subsequently fixed at $5), being at the same time released from the tax on circulation of one per cent. per annum, and the attempt was made to force them to hold a minimum cash reserve against their liabilities, of which a certain percentage must be in legal-tender notes. The principle of a fixed reserve could not be carried, but the banks were required thereafter to hold in legal tenders a certain percentage of whatever reserve they did maintain.

With the power to provide all of the change-making notes of the country, and with the conviction that the banks must steadily hold in their reserves a considerable proportion of the issue, the Government felt safe in fixing the maximum of legal tenders, for the time being, at $9,000,000—an increase of $1,000,000 over the old provincial issue. The regulations with regard to reserves to be held by the Government were slightly altered. The portion covered by debentures was not to exceed eighty per cent., and specie must be held to cover the balance, with a provision that the proportion of specie must not go below fifteen per cent. Issues above $9,000,000 were to be covered entirely by specie.

There were other important discussions and some minor changes in principle, but, in the main, the way was paved for the adoption, pretty much as they stood, of the body of banking laws hitherto in force in the old province of Canada. In 1870, such an act was passed, but permitting the charter of a bank to be renewed by the Governor-in-Council on a report from the Minister of Justice and the Treasury Board assenting thereto. This was not regarded favorably by the banks, who preferred that Parliament should deal with the renewals as well as with the granting of charters. They also desired that regulations for the internal management of banks should be made uniform, and the Act of 1871, covering and thus extending the Act of 1870, was the result. It provided that all banks working under provincial charters might, when such charters expired, come under the Dominion Act, and that all charters under the Dominion Act should expire in 1881. Several special provisions had to be made to cover the few banks whose constitutions were not in accord with the majority of the provincial banks, but, as far as possible, an harmonious system was established. The practice was thus fairly settled, although not, we believe, asserted as a principle, of a decennial revision of the Bank Act accompanying decennial renewals of charters, and in 1880 and 1890 these revisions have taken place. In the interval, Parliament has made such changes as seemed expedient, although the implied agreement with the banks may be presumed to be that no radical changes will be made except at these decennial revisions.

Hitherto it has been convenient to follow events pretty much in their chronological sequence. But, since confederation in 1867, the growth of banking in volume, and the incidents of success and failure connected therewith, are not only quite beyond the scope of the present history, but have no special relation to its purpose, except in so far as they affect the principles with which it deals. The simplest plan, and that, we think, most agreeable to the reader, will therefore be to direct, without further remarks, his careful attention to the subjoined abstract of the present Dominion Bank Act, that of 1890. Every effort has been made to condense the matter and to avoid technical language, and it is hoped that, in connection with the explanatory pages which follow, it will set forth the principles of the act more clearly than a direct examination of the act itself.

ABSTRACT OF THE BANK ACT

53 VICTORIA, CHAPTER 31, ASSENTED TO MAY 16, 1890, TO COME IN FORCE JULY 1, 1891

STATUTE OF DOMINION OF CANADA

SECTIONS 1, 2. TITLE AND INTERPRETATION CLAUSES

APPLICATION OF ACT

Secs. 3, 4. Apply to thirty-six banks enumerated in Schedule A, and any banks incorporated in future, continuing all such charters until July 1, 1901, subject to provisions of this General Bank Act.

Secs. 5, 6, 7, 8. Special provisions for three banks, included in the thirty-six, whose charters differ materially from all other Canadian banks, and for one not included in the thirty-six, the provincial charter of which, granted before confederation, had not at this time expired. (This bank is now working under the act.)

INCORPORATION AND ORGANIZATION

Sec. 9. Act of Incorporation, for which form is supplied (Schedule B), must declare the name of bank, capital stock, place of chief office, and names of provisional directors.

Sec. 10. The capital stock of any bank hereafter must be not less than $500,000, with shares divided into $100 each.

Sec. 11. There must be not less than five nor more than ten provisional directors, who are to hold office until subscribers elect directors in accordance with act.

Sec. 12. Provisional directors may, after public notice, open stock-books for subscription of shares.

Sec. 13. When $500,000 has been *bona fide* subscribed, and not less than $250,000 actually paid to the Minister of Finance and Receiver-General, the provisional directors may, after four weeks' public notice, hold first meeting of subscribers, at which meeting the subscribers shall elect qualified directors to the number of not less than five nor more than ten, replacing provisional directors, and name the date of annual meetings.

Sec. 14. Nothing in the nature of the business of banking shall be transacted until the regular board of directors shall have applied for and obtained a certificate from the Treasury Board permitting the bank to commence business. Breach of this constitutes an offence against the act. (See later as to punishment for offences against the act.)

Secs. 15, 16. Treasury Board shall not issue such certificate until all requirements of this act, and the special Act of Incorporation, have been fulfilled, especially as to the deposit of actual cash, to an amount not less than $250,000, having been made and still being in the hands of the Minister of Finance and Receiver-General. If certificate not issued before one year after passing of Act of Incorporation, all rights lapse.

Sec. 17. Upon issue of certificate, Minister of Finance and Receiver-General pays back all moneys deposited.

INTERNAL REGULATIONS

Sec. 18. The shareholders may (instead of the directors) pass by-laws regarding the following matters:

Date of Annual General Meeting at which shareholders elect directors.

Regulations (subject to limitations mentioned in act) as to proxies, number, quorum, qualification, remuneration, etc., of directors.

Limit of loans or discounts to directors, or to any one person, firm, corporation, or to shareholders.

Authority to establish and contribute to guarantee and pension funds.

Secs. 19, 20. Affairs of bank intrusted to board of directors, eligible for re-election, who are elected annually by shareholders, subject to provisions regarding the minimum qualification in stock-holding, the proportion to be British subjects and the manner of election.

Secs. 21, 22, 23. Provide for chairmanship of board, by-laws by directors, employment of bank officers, and that these shall give security for faithful performance of duties.

Sec. 24. Provides for special general meetings, removal of president or director, etc.

Sec. 25. As to manner of voting by shareholders.

CAPITAL STOCK

Secs. 26, 27. Manner of increasing capital stock and allotting shares.

Sec. 28. Manner of reducing capital stock.

Secs. 29 to 34, inclusive. Manner of subscribing for shares, making calls thereupon, etc.

Secs. 35 to 44, inclusive. Manner of transfer and transmission of shares.

ANNUAL STATEMENT

Sec. 45. At annual meeting directors must submit clear and full statement of affairs (see act for details).

Sec. 46. Books, correspondence, funds, etc., at all times subject to inspection by directors.

DIVIDENDS (PROFITS)

Sec. 47. Dividends, unless not earned, to be declared not less often than half-yearly.

Sec. 48. Directors who knowingly join in declaring dividend or bonus which impairs paid up capital shall be jointly and severally liable therefor.

If capital is impaired, directors shall make calls upon shareholders to make good such impairment. Net profits must be applied for same purpose.

Sec. 49. No dividend or bonus, or both combined, exceeding eight per cent. per annum shall be paid unless the net rest fund, or surplus profit reserved, exceeds thirty per cent. of the paid-up capital.

RESERVES

Sec. 50. Of the cash reserves held by a bank (the proportion of such reserves to liabilities being entirely at the bank's discretion) not less than forty per cent. shall be in legal-tender notes of the Dominion of Canada. Penalty for non-compliance $500 for each violation.

NOTE ISSUES

Sec. 51. Banks may issue notes payable to bearer, on demand, and intended for circulation. No note smaller than $5, and all notes to be multiples of $5. Total issue shall not exceed the unimpaired paid-up capital. (A sub-section further limits the issues of two of the banks referred to in Sections 5 to 8 inclusive.)

The following are the penalties for issues in excess of the amount authorized by this act :

Excess not over $1,000. Penalty equal to excess.

Over $	1,000	but	not	over $	20,000.	Penalty $	1,000.
"	20,000	"	"	"	100,000.	"	10,000.
"	100,000	"	"	"	200,000.	"	50,000.
"	200,000					"	100,000.

Sec. 52. Bank shall not pledge its notes, and no loan thereon shall be recoverable from a bank. Any director or officer concerned in the pledging of a bank's notes, and any person receiving such notes as security, shall be liable to fine, not less than $400 nor more than $2,000, or imprisonment for not more than two years, or both.

Similar clause regarding fraudulent issue of notes, penalty being imprisonment for term not exceeding seven years, or fine not exceeding $2,000, or both.

Sec. 53. Note issues are a first charge on the assets of the bank in case of insolvency; any debt due to the Dominion Government a second charge; and any debt to the Government of any province a third charge. Any debt due the Dominion Government at the time of insolvency for penalties under the act not payable until all other liabilities are paid.

THE BANK CIRCULATION REDEMPTION FUND

Sec. 54. Each bank shall maintain with the Minister of Finance and Receiver-General a deposit "equal to five per cent. of the average amount of its notes in circulation" for the twelve months prior to the preceding 1st July.

These deposits shall constitute "The Bank Circulation Redemption Fund," which shall be held only for the purpose of redeeming the notes of banks which fail to redeem their issues in specie or legal tenders, and any interest due thereon. For all notes so redeemed the fund shall have the same rights against the estate of the failed bank as any other holder. The Government shall allow interest on the fund at three per cent. per annum. (A sub-section provides the manner of ascertaining the average circulation of each bank.)

If a bank suspends payment of its notes, interest accrues thereafter at six per cent. per annum, until a day named for their redemption, of which public notice must be given by the liquidator or other officer in charge; after which, so long as redemption of all issues presented is maintained, further interest on notes outstanding ceases. If, after the expiration of two months from date of suspension, the liquidator is not prepared to redeem, the Minister of Finance and Receiver-General may redeem out of the fund, after notice, whereupon interest ceases.

If payments made from the fund exceed the contributions of the particular bank whose notes are so redeemed, the remaining contributors shall recoup the fund *pro rata* to the amount at credit of each with the fund, for such excess, recoveries from the estate of the failed bank being of course distributed among such contributors in like proportion. Provided that no bank shall be required to pay in any one year more than one per cent. calculated on its average circulation.

In the winding up of a bank and upon satisfactory arrangements being made for the redemption of all outstanding notes with interest, the Treasury Board may return the sum at credit of the bank with the fund, or such part of it as may seem expedient.

The Treasury Board may make rules and regulations for the management of the fund.

The Minister of Finance and Receiver-General may take legal action to enforce payment of any sum due by a bank under this section.

Sec. 55. Banks are required to ensure the circulation of their notes at par in every part of Canada. This is at present effected by requiring each bank to have known redemption agents in the cities of chief commercial importance in each province, of which seven are named in the act.

Sec. 56. Although the notes of a bank are almost invariably payable only at its head office, its notes must be received in payment of debts at any of its establishments.

Sec. 57. In making a payment, a bank must, if required, provide Dominion legal tenders in denominations of one, two and four dollars, not exceeding one hundred dollars in any one payment. No payment in legal tender or bank notes shall be made in torn or partially defaced notes.

Sec. 58. Provides that obligations under seal of the bank may be assignable by the indorsement of the person to whom made payable. Notes of issue to be binding without the seal of the bank, and may be assigned without indorsement. Proviso as to who may be authorised to sign notes of issue for the directors.

Sec. 59. Authorises engraved signatures, provided there is at least one authorised written signature on each note.

Sec. 60. Penalty for issue of notes to pass as money except by a bank, and as to what shall be deemed such notes.

Sec. 61. Penalty for defacing legal tenders or bank notes.

Sec. 62. Instructions to officers receiving public moneys and to bank officers and bankers' employees to stamp or write on fraudulent legal tenders or bank notes, such words as "counterfeit," "altered," or "worthless," in accordance with the fact.

Sec. 63. Penalty for issuing advertisements in the form of legal tenders or bank notes.

BUSINESS AND POWERS OF THE BANK

Sec. 64. The bank may open *branches*, *agencies* and *offices*, and may engage in and carry on business as a dealer in gold and silver coin and bullion, and it may deal in, discount and lend money and make advances upon the security of, and may take as collateral security for any loan made by it, bills of exchange, promissory notes and other negotiable securities, or the stock, bonds, debentures and obligations of municipal and other corporations, whether secured by mortgage or otherwise, or Dominion, Provincial, British, foreign and other public securities, and it may engage in and carry on such business generally as appertains to the business of banking; but, except as authorised by this act, it shall not, either directly or indirectly, deal in the buying or selling, or bartering of goods, wares and merchandise, or engage or be engaged in any trade or business whatsoever; and it shall not, either directly or indirectly, purchase, or deal in, or lend money, or make advances upon the security or pledge of any share of its own capital stock, or of the capital stock of any bank; and it shall not, either directly or indirectly, lend money or make advances upon the security, mortgage or hypothecation of any land, tenements or immovable property, or of any ships or other vessels, or upon the security of any goods, wares and merchandise. (Quoted in full.)

Sec. 65. A bank has a privileged lien on shares of its own stock held by a debtor, or on dividends thereon, for any debt or liability of shareholder. Provision as to when bank may sell after default, and how to transfer title.

Sec. 66. Similar provision for sale of collateral securities when no agreement as to power of sale has been made.

Sec. 67. Bank may hold real property for its own use and occupation.

Sec. 68. Bank may take for a debt already contracted additional security by mortgage on real or personal property.

Sec. 69. Bank may purchase real property sold under execution, etc., provided it already has a lien thereon as security for a debt.

Sec. 70. Bank may acquire title to real property on which it has a lien as security, by acquiring equity or by foreclosure. But no bank shall hold real property, except for its own use and occupation, longer than seven years.

Sec. 71. General clause confirming right of banks to hold real property and to convey same.

Sec. 72. Gives power to advance money for building ships and to take such security thereon as private individuals are permitted to take.

Sec. 73. Gives power to advance on ordinary warehouse receipts and bills of lading.

Sec. 74. (1) The bank may lend money to any person engaged in business as a wholesale manufacturer of any goods, wares and merchandise upon the security of the goods, wares and merchandise manufactured by him or procured for such manufacture ;

(2) The bank may also lend money to any wholesale purchaser or shipper of products of agriculture, the forest and mine, or the sea, lakes and rivers, or to any wholesale purchaser or shipper of live stock or dead stock, and the products thereof, upon the security of such products, or of such live stock or dead stock, and the products thereof ;

(3) Such security may be given by the owner and may be taken in the form set forth in Schedule C to this act, or to the like effect ; and by virtue of such security, the bank shall acquire the same rights and powers in respect to the goods, wares and merchandise, stock or products covered thereby, as if it had acquired the same by virtue of a warehouse receipt. (Quoted in full.)

Sec. 75. Bank may not hold warehouse receipt or bill of lading under Section 73, or pledge under Section 74, unless acquired at time of making loan, or unless a promise to give same was acquired or held at time of making loan. May exchange warehouse receipt, bill of lading or pledge for any other form of lien on the same goods. Penalty for false statement in warehouse receipt, bill of lading or pledge, or for alienating or removing goods covered by warehouse receipt, bill of lading or pledge, imprisonment not exceeding two years.

Sec. 76. Material or goods on which bank has a lien by warehouse receipt or pledge may be converted by manufacture without the bank losing its lien.

Sec. 77. All advances so secured under Sections 73 and 74 shall have priority to the claim of an unpaid vendor, unless he had a lien on such goods of which the bank was aware.

Sec. 78. How power of sale, in case of default, shall be exercised.

Sec. 79. Penalty to a bank violating any of Sections 64 to 78 inclusive, a sum not exceeding $500.

Sec. 80. Bank not liable to any penalty or forfeiture for usury. May stipulate for and recover, or may take in advance, any rate not over seven per cent.

Sec. 81. No negotiable instrument to be void on ground of usury.

Sec. 82. Bank in discounting bills payable at its own branches may not take commission in addition to interest beyond the following rates: Bills under thirty days, one-eighth of one per cent.; thirty or over, but under sixty, one-fourth of one per cent.; sixty or over, but under ninety, three-eighths of one per cent.; ninety days and over, one-half of one per cent.

Sec. 83. Bank in discounting bills payable at points where it has no branches may charge a commission, not exceeding in any case one-half of one per cent.

Sec. 84. Bank may receive deposits from any person, whether qualified by law to contract or not, and may repay unless the money is lawfully claimed by another. Proviso that deposits under this authority shall not in any one case exceed $500.

Bank shall not be bound to see to the execution of any trust in relation to such deposits.

RETURNS BY BANKS TO GOVERNMENT

Sec. 85. *Monthly Returns*: Banks must send to the Minister of Finance and Receiver-General a statement to the close of each month. (This return, the form of which will be found at Schedule D of the act, covers a very full statement of assets and liabilities under uniform headings, and is published in the Government Gazette.) Penalty, $50 per day for each day's delay after 15th of subsequent month.

Sec. 86. *Special Returns*: The Minister of Finance and Receiver-General may call for special returns at any time. Penalty, after thirty days, $300 per day, unless the Minister of Finance extends the time.

Sec. 87. *List of Shareholders*: At the close of the calendar year each bank must supply to the Minister of Finance and Receiver-General a list of shareholders, with addresses and number of shares held. Penalty, $50 a day after twenty days.

Sec. 88. *Unclaimed Moneys*: At the close of the calendar year banks must make to the Minister of Finance and Receiver-General a statement of dividends and all other amounts which have been unclaimed, or regarding which there have been no transactions for five years, giving names and addresses in full. Penalty, $50 per day after twenty days.

The liquidator of a bank, after three years, shall pay over to the Minister of Finance and Receiver-General all such amounts remaining unclaimed, together with all interest due, and the Government shall hold these in trust for the owners, continuing interest, where this was contracted for by the bank, at three per cent. per annum.

The liquidator of a bank shall, also, after three years, pay to the Minister of Finance and Receiver-General an amount equal to the outstanding circulation to be held by the Government in trust for the holders of such notes.

INSOLVENCY

Sec. 89. If the assets are insufficient to meet the liabilities, shareholders, in addition to their liability upon unpaid shares, are liable for further payments to an amount equal to the par value of shares held.

Sec. 90. The liability of a bank for any moneys deposited, or dividends declared, continues notwithstanding any statute of limitations.

Sec. 91. Suspension for ninety days, either consecutively or at intervals during twelve months, constitutes insolvency, and forfeits charter, except for purposes of liquidation.

Secs. 92, 93 and 94. Manner of making and enforcing calls authorized by Section 89.

Sec. 95. As to liabilities of directors in event of failure.

Sec. 96. Shareholders do not escape liability under Section 89, unless shares transferred more than sixty days prior to suspension of payment.

OFFENCES AND PENALTIES

Sec. 97. Any director or officer giving undue preference in any manner to any creditor of a bank is subject to imprisonment for term not exceeding two years.

Sec. 98. All penalties collected for violation of this act shall be for public uses of Canada, with power to Governor-in-Council to make exceptions.

Sec. 99. Any director or officer willfully making or signing a false return or statement of bank's affairs is subject to imprisonment for term not exceeding five years, unless the offence is more serious than a misdemeanor under the act.

Sec. 100. Forbidding the use of the title "bank," "banking company," "banking house," "banking association," or "banking institution," unless authorised by this act.

Sec. 101. Everything declared to be an "offence against this act" liable to fine not exceeding $1,000, or imprisonment not exceeding five years, or both.

PUBLIC NOTICES

Sec. 102. All public notices required by act shall, unless otherwise specified, be advertised in one or more newspapers where head office is situated, and in "Canada Gazette."

Sec. 103 Banks must cash at par all official cheques of any department of the Dominion Government.

Sec. 104. Declares that act shall come into force July 1, 1891, and repeals other acts.

Schedule A. Names of thirty six banks whose charters are continued.
" B. Form of Act of Incorporation of new banks.
" C. " Security under Section 74.
" D. " Monthly return to Government.

CHAPTER V

SCOPE OF EXISTING LAWS

TERM OF CHARTER—INTERNAL REGULATIONS—CIRCULATION—BUSINESS AND POWERS—PENALTIES, ETC.

BY Section 4 of the Banking Act, the charters of all banks existing at the time of its enactment are extended for ten years, or until July 1, 1901, while the charter of any new bank created during the period expires at the same time. Thus the life of a bank, apparently, is only ten years, and as all charters come to an end at the same time, it might be possible for the country to be suddenly left without any authorized banks. Practically, the results are in every way beneficial. Bankers, as a rule, think the period too short; and now that the principles of Canadian banking appear to be firmly settled, the period might reasonably be extended to twenty years. It is the effect of all charters expiring together to which the reader's attention is asked. This arrangement ensures a complete review of the principles underlying the act, and of the details connected with the working of it, once in ten years. In the interval the banks are almost free from attempts by demagogues or ambitious but ill-informed legislators to interfere with the details of the system; but during the session of Parliament preceding the date of the expiry of the charters they must defend the system against the demagogue, the bank-hater, the honest but inexperienced citizen who writes letters to the press, sometimes the press itself—indeed, against all the kinds of attack to which institutions possessing a franchise granted by the people are subject when they come before the public to answer for their stewardship. But while resisting the attacks of ignorance, they are, of course, called upon to answer such just criticism as may arise from the existence of defects in their system made evident by the experiences of time. Or, perhaps, as when the act was under discussion in 1890, they may see the defects even more clearly than the public, and may themselves suggest the remedies. Whatever may be said for or against these decennial contests, the product of each discussion is a banking act improved in many respects by the exchange of opinion between the bankers and the public. The banking system is thus brought at each period of renewal to a higher degree of perfection through having been subjected to unsparing analysis by an unusually enlightened people—perhaps too democratic in tendency and too jealous of every privilege granted, but anxious to build rather than to destroy.

INCORPORATION

There is a peculiar charm in the ownership of a corporation which owes its existence and its privileges to a special Act of Legislature, and if its privileges cover anything in the nature of a monopoly the charm is heightened. In Canada, we have had one section of the people who have been so enamored of freedom that they have desired to see banking as well as other privileges reduced to the mere necessity of applying for incorporation under a general act, together with the subscription of the smallest amount of capital which it seemed possible to propose. But, as a rule, people of British origin want merely all the liberty which is compatible with freedom from license. So that while, in the main, Parliament has clung to its prerogative of refusing a charter if it chose to do so, during fifty years at least, it would not have dared to exercise the power except in the event of a clearly fraudulent application for a charter. Nor would it dare, although it has the power, to give special privileges to any one bank. In the United States, a certain number of individuals having complied with certain requirements—more numerous and complicated, by the way, than the Canadian requirements—become thereby an incorporated bank, if we regard the consent of the Comptroller of Currency as a matter of form. In Canada, when a certain number of individuals have complied with certain requirements, they are supposed to have applied for a charter, which Parliament theoretically might refuse, but which, as a matter of fact, would not be refused unless doubt existed as to the *bona fide* character of the proposed bank. Then, as in the United States, on complying with certain other requirements and obtaining consent of the Treasury Board (performing in this case the same function as the Comptroller of Currency in the United States), the bank is ready for business.

What has given Canadians more concern than the manner of incorporation is the means of determining that each proposed bank is a genuine business venture, with enough capital at the back of it to ensure this fact, and to warrant the extension to it of the franchise of issuing notes against its general estate. As early as 1834, a New Brunswick act, adopting the recommendations of the Committee for Trade, already referred to, required that public commissioners should count the cash in the possession of a proposed bank in order to ascertain if the actual capital had been paid in, and that no notes should be issued until one-half of the capital was actually paid in. But there was no requirement as to a minimum capital, and in the case of the particular bank to which the act applied the amount paid up was very small indeed. Nor was there any time fixed for the payment of the remainder of the subscribed capital. In the report of the first committee on banking and currency appointed after the union of Lower and Upper Canada in 1841, it was recommended that the amount of capital be fixed (Parliament presumably to judge in each case as to what was sufficient), and the whole to be subscribed within eighteen months from the date of the charter; the bank was not to begin business until the whole was subscribed and one-half paid up, and the whole must be paid up within two years from date of charter. In the year after confederation, that is, in 1868, the committee on banking and currency received, it will be remembered, certain advice from prominent bankers and others. One of the recommendations was that a minimum of capital to be subscribed be named, and that whatever portion had by law to be paid up before business was commenced should be certified to by a Government official as held in specie. When in 1870 the first discussion of the principles of an act took place, the Minister of Finance wished this minimum to be placed at $1,000,000, with at least $200,000 paid in before business was transacted, the balance to be paid at the rate of twenty per cent. each year. After discussion the minimum was fixed at $500,000, of which $200,000 should be paid before business was transacted. But this was modified next year to a requirement that only $100,000 be paid up at the commencement and another $100,000 within two years. It was about this time that the three largest banks increased their capital to $12,000,000, $9,000,000 and $6,000,000, respectively; and while these were figures quite unnecessarily large, the contrast with some of the banks, which had been allowed to come into existence under provincial charters with a capital of $100,000 or $200,000, was very great indeed. It will be seen that in the Act of 1890 (Sections 10, 13, 15 and 16) the conditions are more stringent than at any previous time; and notwithstanding the rapid growth of democratic sentiment, the disposition of the country appears to be now pretty much settled against the creation of small banks. The *bona fide* subscription of $500,000 of stock must be secured, and of this $250,000 must be at once paid up, and the actual cash placed temporarily with the Minister of Finance and Receiver-General, before the final certificate is obtained to the effect that all the conditions required by law have been complied with. In the history of Canada, as in other new countries, the placing of the capital stock of new banks has been accompanied by all sorts of abuses. The so-called "cash" with which a bank has begun business has sometimes turned out to be largely composed of shareholders' notes of hand, or any one of many other devices has been resorted to to make a "brave outside" for the public to look at. No restrictions will altogether prevent the occurrence of some form of deception; but, without doubt, the present conditions are most carefully devised in order that it may be reasonably certain that each new bank authorized by Parliament will be an honest business venture.

INTERNAL REGULATIONS

The regulations concerning the relations between the shareholders and the directors set forth in Sections 18 to 25, inclusive, are, with a few exceptions, such as might be adopted in the management of any large corporation, and have therefore little value in connection with a study of the practice of banking. That the directors should not have power to remunerate themselves, except under authority of the shareholders (Sec. 18), was a provision of the earliest charter in old Canada—that granted to the Bank of Montreal in 1821, several years after it commenced business. That the directors, or a majority, shall be British subjects (Sec. 19), and that directors shall be responsible for the employment of bank officers, and shall require them to give security for faithful service (Sec. 23), were also features of the same charter. The matter of loans to directors has always been, and still is, a difficult question, for which no more satisfactory solution has been found than to permit comparative freedom, except that in the monthly return the aggregate of loans to directors must be shown. In the recommendations of the Committee for Trade, it was provided that directors were not to borrow more than one-third of the total amount lent by the bank. This was adopted by New Brunswick as early as 1834, with the proportion applied to the capital of the bank instead of to the total amount lent. But as one bank has $12,000,000 of capital while another may have $500,000, such an attempt at limitation would now be worse than useless. We have not got further than to empower shareholders, by passing a by-law to such effect, to restrain the board of directors to the extent that they see fit in making such loans. Two points in this connection are clear. If a bank has a board consisting entirely of directors who do not borrow, it runs great risk of not being in touch with the active business community; because until Canada is a much richer country, the business men still in the prime of life are likely to be borrowers. On the other hand, as long as directors are allowed to borrow from the bank at whose board they have a seat, there will be losses, and, occasionally, losses not justifiable.

Under Section 18, banks may establish and contribute to funds in order to insure the fidelity and provide for the superannuation of their officers, or otherwise assist the families of their officers. In the majority of banks, officers are no longer permitted to secure their fidelity by bonds of private individuals, and instead of purchasing insurance from the ordinary fidelity or guarantee companies, several banks have funds of their own, created by contributions from both bank and officers. This might not be practicable in a very small bank, but it has proved absolutely successful for many years past in some of the large banks. Pension funds, based generally upon the system in use in the British and Canadian Civil Services, are in operation in several banks.

Section 19 opens by stating that "The stock, property, affairs and concerns of the bank shall be managed by a board of directors, etc." Management "by a board of directors" is, of course, a phrase of very variable meaning; and in Canada it ranges from the practice of a large English or Scotch bank, where the oversight of the board is very general indeed, to that of some American banks where the board really may be said to manage the bank directly and where the president is actually the chief executive officer. There are no longer in Canada special "discount days" on which the board sits and discusses the bills offered. It is necessary now to empower the agent at the smallest branch, by instructions given in advance, to transact the business of his established customers. New customers, if proposing important business, must await the decision of the board, but old ones, if in good standing, are not usually willing to do so. The board, as a rule, sits once a week, and is asked to approve of the more important lines of credit. The president may be in such close touch that he knows the business almost as well as the general manager; but this, as a rule, he cannot be, and the latter is the real chief executive officer. The president, however, is in daily contact with the general management, and is fully able to judge as to whether the bank is being soundly and honestly managed, while the board, by the nature of the business discussed every week, should also be in a position to know whether the affairs of the bank are prospering or not. More than this is impossible on the part of a board of directors in the present complicated nature of the business of a large bank.

Section 25 contains six sub-sections covering elaborate provisions as to voting at shareholders' meetings, for information regarding which we must refer readers to the actual text of the act. In the earliest acts, voting was arranged by a scale, so that while one share gave one vote, ten shares gave only five and thirty shares only ten, while no holding gave more than twenty votes. This practice was considered fair, and was followed in many charters; but in granting new charters in 1855, the Legislature of old Canada changed this to the practice which has been followed since—of one vote for each share.

CAPITAL STOCK

Sections 26 and 27 deal with the manner of increasing and allotting capital stock, and 28 with the reduction of capital. The capital can neither be increased nor decreased except by the consent of a majority of the shareholders, obtained at an annual or special meeting, and the subsequent consent of the Treasury Board. New or unsubscribed stock (Sec. 27) must be allotted *pro rata*, and any premium fixed thereon must not exceed the percentage which the reserve fund (surplus) bears to the paid-up capital stock. The consent of the Treasury Board cannot be obtained to a reduction of the capital until statements of the condition of the bank setting forth "the reasons and causes why such reduction is sought" are submitted. The reduction of the capital stock in the manner indicated does not diminish the liability of the shareholders to the creditors of the bank existing before such reduction is formally legalized. The capital stock cannot be reduced, if the bank remains in business, below the sum of $250,000.

Sections 29 to 44, inclusive, deal with the following subjects: subscription for shares (29); payment of calls on new shares (30 and 31); enforcement of same (32, 33 and 34); conditions under which shares may be transferred (35); provision that a list of transfers shall be made daily and exhibited for information of shareholders (36); provision to prevent the selling of stock by others than the actual owners, such as the sale of shares not owned, with the expectation of purchasing later at a lower price (37); manner of transferring shares sold under execution (38); in cases of death, bankruptcy, insolvency, or marriage of female shareholder (39, 40, 41 and 42); provision that bank is not bound to see to the execution of trusts (43); provision that executors and trustees shall not, when the real owner is indicated in the books of the bank, be subject personally to liability on the shares so standing in their names as executors or trustees—if the actual owner is living and competent, he is liable as if the shares stood in his name, and if dead or incompetent, his estate is liable (44). The sixteen sections here referred to are very lengthy and are elaborately worked out, but have little to do with the study of banking. One provision, however, may interest bankers in the United States. It is imperative, under Section 35, that the transferee of shares shall actually accept the same on the books of the bank, in person or by attorney, and thus formally admit his double liability.

ANNUAL STATEMENT—DIVIDENDS

The very natural provisions in Sections 45 to 49, inclusive, call for little comment. Sections 45, 46, 47 and 48 were substantially included in the first charter granted (1821), while the principle of Section 49 was covered by the recommendations of the bankers made to the committee on banking and currency (1868-69).

CASH RESERVES

When the Government abandoned hope of creating a bank of issue or a national currency, it imposed, as will be remembered, upon the banks the condition that they must carry in their reserves a certain percentage of legal-tender notes of the Dominion. This is a distinct blot upon the Banking Act; but as the banks carry much more than the percentage required, it probably might now be removed from the act without causing the Government inconvenience. In its early years, the Dominion had its credit to establish, and was called upon to make expenditures in public works, at a very heavy cost, for a new and sparsely settled country, and it was obliged to resort to several financial expedients which with its present high credit would be not only unnecessary but very unwise.

It will also be remembered that, in proposing this feature, the Minister of Finance coupled with it the requirement that banks should hold a minimum cash reserve against all liabilities. This was strenuously objected to by the bankers and was not insisted upon. In the revision of the act in 1890, the Government again proposed the principle of a minimum reserve, and again the bankers were able by their arguments to demonstrate the unsoundness of such a requirement.

The mere statement of the reserve in cash held by a particular bank, or the average held by the banks of an entire country, conveys little idea as to whether prudence is observed or not. In Canada, the average, for some years, of actual cash held in gold and legal tenders as against all liabilities to the public, is about ten per cent. But, owing to the system of bank note issues, very little of this is required for daily use, the tills of bank offices being filled with the bank's own notes, which do not appear in its statements as cash because they are not in circulation. Practically, the business across the counter, when not transacted with other paper instruments, is served by this till money; the settlements of balances with other banks are made in legal tenders, or by drafts on the chief commercial centres; while the main reserve may be, in the case of small banks, represented by their loans at call or short date on stocks and bonds and by their balances in the hands of correspondents at Montreal and New York. In addition to such sources of strength, the more important banks have agencies in the United States, and the bulk of the capital employed there can be made available without any delay, while practically all can be liquidated within a few months at most.

The Canadian bankers have always been ready to discuss the relative merits of a minimum reserve fixed by law as against perfect freedom to banks in the management of their reserves, the overwhelming majority being in favor of the latter course as the only practicable system if stringency and panic are to be averted.

NOTE ISSUE.

To the foreign reader, Sections 51 to 63, inclusive, are, doubtless, the most interesting in the act. In Canada, we began with the very simple and obvious theory that, without the existence of laws to the contrary, an individual had the right to issue his promise to pay in any form, the only deterrent to the exercise of such a luxury being the difficulty of inducing anyone to accept it in payment. We have seen that, for a considerable period, the law did not interfere with the exercise of this power, and in collections devoted to historical objects many curious specimens of money issued by private business as well as private banking firms may be found. Indeed, in refusing for such a long time to grant the privilege to an incorporated bank, the first Legislature of Lower Canada was, doubtless, moved only by the fear that, because of the express authority of law, the bank might be able to float an undue amount of such money. In the present act, the mere right, apart from subsequent qualifications, is expressed in a few simple words: "The bank may issue and reissue notes payable to bearer on demand and intended for circulation" (Sec. 51).

The first qualification (Sec. 51) is that it must not issue notes of smaller denominations than five dollars, and must issue all notes in multiples of five dollars. The history of this restriction has been given. The Government desired to provide, out of its legal-tender issues, the entire change-making paper currency of the country, and first fixed the lowest note issuable by a bank at $4 (the old currency pound), and subsequently at $5.

Section 51 also provides that the entire circulation of a bank shall not exceed its unimpaired paid-up capital, imposing enormous fines for breaches of the provision; and further limiting to seventy-five per cent. of the capital the notes of two banks having special charters, because in both cases the shareholders are not subject to the double liability. These banks may issue up to the full unimpaired paid-up capital by depositing cash or Government bonds for the amount issued over the seventy-five per cent. In the early banking of a new country, few deposits can be obtained, and the main object of organizing a bank is to secure the privilege of note-issuing, the profit on lending the capital, plus the notes in circulation, being at such a time a sufficient inducement. The first charter (1821), so often referred to, contained no other restriction upon the volume of note issues than that the total of all liabilities to the public must not exceed three times the capital stock actually paid in, the directors being personally liable if they permitted an excess. For many years, this was the general principle followed, although it was varied somewhat in its application and modified in some of the provinces as time went on. We find the bankers who offered suggestions to the banking and currency committee of 1868-69, asking that the power to issue be limited to the paid-up capital, plus Government securities and specie held, but in the legislation which followed it was limited as in Section 51; no limit being placed, however, upon the total liabilities of a bank.

Section 53 makes the note issues a prior lien upon the estate of the bank, prior even to a debt due to the Crown. This was one of the recommendations of the bankers to the banking and currency committee of 1868-69, and it is very much to be regretted that it was not embodied in the first general bank act of the Dominion. But the Minister of Finance failed to recognize the difference between an involuntary holder receiving a note in the course of business and a depositor who selects a particular bank to which he gives credit in the form of his deposit. Between 1874 and 1879 there were serious bank troubles, in some cases ending in failure, and in one case, a particularly discreditable failure, the creditors—note-holders as well as depositors—recovering, after exhausting the double liability, only fifty-seven and one-half cents in the dollar. The bank was of little importance directly, having few notes in circulation, but the result of the liquidation was a great shock. As a consequence, at the revision of 1880 the principle of Section 53 found a place in the act. Thus, while it will always be a matter of regret that any note issued under the laws of the Dominion should not have been eventually paid in full, it is to be remembered that if the views of the bankers expressed in 1869 had been acceded to, the record to-day would show that, without further security than that of being a prior lien upon the general estate, the note issues had been always redeemed in full.

But there were still two minor though serious defects in the system. It was frequently alleged by those who admired the National Bank Act of the United States, that while the currency created by it might not be elastic, the notes could not for any reason fail to be paid in full, and to circulate throughout the entire area of the United States, while in Canada no similar boast could be made. The area of Canada is enormous relatively to population, and the notes of banks in one province certainly passed at a discount in some of the others, a recurrence in a less aggravated form of the defect in the old State-bank issues of the United States. And while it might be confidently asserted that all bank issues secured by being a first lien on the estate of the banks would be eventually paid in full, it was nevertheless true that because of doubt and delay the notes of a suspended bank always fell to a discount for the time being. To meet these two defects, the bankers, in the revision of 1890, proposed the principles set forth in Sections 54 and 55, borrowing their ideas once more from the larger experience of banking in the United States.

The distinctive features, therefore, of the bank note issues of Canada are: They are not secured by the pledge or special deposit with the Government of bonds or other securities, but are simply credit instruments based upon the general assets of the bank issuing them. But in order that they may be not less secure than notes issued against bonds deposited with the Government, they are made a first charge upon the assets (Sec. 53).

To avoid discount at the moment of the suspension of a bank, either because of delay in payment of note issues by the liquidator or of doubt as to ultimate payment, each bank is obliged to keep in the hands of the Government a deposit equal to five per cent. on its average circulation, the average being taken from the maximum circulation of each bank in each month of the year. This is called the Bank Circulation Redemption Fund, and should any liquidator fail to redeem the note of a failed bank, recourse may be had to the entire fund if necessary. As a matter of fact, liquidators are almost invariably able to redeem the note issues as they are presented, but in order that all solvent banks may accept without loss the notes of an insolvent bank, these notes bear six per cent. interest from the date of suspension to the date of the liquidator's announcement that he is ready to redeem (Sec. 54).

To avoid discount, for geographical reasons each bank is obliged to arrange for the redemption of its notes in the commercial centres throughout the Dominion (Sec. 55).

The remaining sections, 52 and 56 to 63, inclusive, require no comment.

BUSINESS AND POWERS OF THE BANK

Under this heading there are twenty-one sections in the act, containing about 330 lines, as compared with a few lines in the first charter. The disposition of Canadian bankers in earlier times was to assume that they had power to do anything in the nature of banking not prohibited by their charter or by the general Bank Act, if there was one. Now, however, the act is broad enough to leave no doubt. In Section 64 it expressly permits branches and agencies, without any condition as to whether they are to be confined to Canada or not, and, while it tries to describe fully the business of banking, it ends the description with a phrase wide enough to include any species of banking not directly prohibited in the act itself. The section covers three prohibitions, two of which appear in the first charter (1821). A bank must not engage in any species of business except banking, and it must not lend money on the security of real estate or other real property. The third provision, to the effect that a bank must not lend on its own stock, was one of the recommendations of the Committee for Trade, and was adopted by New Brunswick in a charter granted in 1832. For a few years, the provision was relaxed under Dominion legislation, but it was again enforced, and is now regarded as a principle firmly fixed in the act.

Section 65 gives a bank a first lien on shares of its own stock, or any dividend due thereon, when the stock is owned by a debtor. This also appeared in the first charter (1821). With the system of transferring shares in the United States such a lien might work unjustly, but in Canada it is a very natural provision which cannot operate unfairly to any third party. No stock certificate, as the phrase is understood in the United States, is ever given by a bank. A holder may obtain, if he so desires, a certificate which is generally called a "stock certificate," but which simply asserts that he owns so many shares transferable only on the books of the bank. Under no circumstances is he called upon to return this document. It is a mere letter of advice upon which no one would lend anything.

Section 67 contains the usual provision that a bank may hold real property for its own use; and 68, that although it cannot lend on real property, it may take such to secure a debt already contracted. It cannot, however, through the medium of Section 76, practically secure real estate for a new advance, the decisions being quite clear that there must have been no agreement or understanding when the loan was made that the real estate was to be given as security for it.

Sections 66, 69, 70 and 71 merely enable banks to realize on securities pledged to them or to complete their title to same.

Section 72 came into operation at a time when it was thought desirable to facilitate ship-building, but to the writer it seems very doubtful banking. In any event, it is probably not of much avail in these days, iron ship-building having nearly ended wooden ship-building in our maritime provinces.

Section 73 confirms the ordinary power of lending on warehouse receipts and bills of lading. A warehouse receipt upon which a bank in Canada is allowed to lend money, must be given by someone other than the owner of the goods.

Sections 74 to 79, inclusive, give facilities to banks not enjoyed by private money-lenders. In early days, when banks were called upon to lend large sums for the moving to market of raw products, the manufacture of lumber, etc., it was strongly felt that there was the need of some simple means by which the title in the property thus purchased or manufactured with its money could be held by the bank. In 1859, in old Canada, a banking bill was passed mainly to facilitate commercial transactions and giving the powers indicated above. While the principle has been extended since, the main features of the present act are not essentially different. The courts having decided that the warehouseman giving a receipt upon which a bank might lend money must be a bailee and not the owner of the goods warehoused, the principle was extended in 1861 so as to cover certain cases in which the warehouseman was also the owner. The Dominion Act adopted this legislation with little change, but the last act, that of 1890, alters the form of procedure when advances are being made upon the security of goods in the owner's possession, and banks are given power in such cases to take a direct pledge upon raw and manufactured products to the extent set forth in Section 74, which is quoted without abbreviation.

The reader who desires to study fully these sections is referred to a paper entitled "Warehouse Receipts, Bills of Lading, and Securities under Section 74 of the Bank Act," read by Mr. Z. A. Lash, counsel for the Canadian Bankers' Association, at its annual meeting in 1894, and published in the journal of the Association, volume ii, page 54.

Sections 80 to 83, inclusive, are certainly not very creditable. Prior to 1858, usury laws existed in Canada, and these sections are an inheritance from that period. For all practical purposes, they might as well be stricken from the act. In 1853, while the law only permitted the collection of six per cent. per annum interest, the penalty for receiving more was removed; but this did not apply to banks or land mortgage companies. In 1858, the right to contract for any rate was given, but again not to banks, except that they might take seven instead of six per cent., with such provisions as are indicated in Sections 82 and 83 as to commissions.

The Dominion Act repeats these provisions with little change, except the important one that all banks are now free from penalty for usury (Secs. 80 and 81). For fuller information regarding the history of Canadian usury laws and of the present legal rate of interest where no contract has been made, the reader is referred to an article in the third volume of the "Journal of the Canadian Bankers' Association," page 377, entitled "The Legal Rate of Interest."

STATEMENTS BY BANKS TO GOVERNMENT

From the simple provision in the first charter that the Government might at any time require for the protection of the public a statement under oath of the position of a bank to the last revision in 1890, there has been a steady amplification of the information given by banks to the public. The nature of the present monthly returns (Sec. 85) cannot be better indicated than by the subjoined list giving the forms of the headings of the various columns:

ASSETS	LIABILITIES
Specie.	
Dominion Notes.	To the Public
Deposits with Dominion Government for security of note circulation.	Notes in circulation.
Notes of and cheques on other banks.	
Loans to other banks in Canada, secured.	Balance due to Dominion Government, after deducting advances for credits, pay lists, etc.
Deposits, payable on demand or after notice, or on a fixed day, made with other banks in Canada.	Balance due to provincial governments.
Balances due from other banks in Canada in daily exchanges.	
Balances due from agencies of the bank, or from other banks or agencies in foreign countries.	Deposits by the public, payable on demand.
Balances due from agencies of the bank, or from other banks or agencies in the United Kingdom.	Deposits by the public, payable after notice or on a fixed day.
Dominion Government debentures or stocks.	Loans from other banks in Canada, secured.

STATEMENTS BY BANKS TO GOVERNMENT—*Continued*

ASSETS—*Continued*

Canadian municipal securities, and British, provincial, or foreign, or colonial, public securities (other than Dominion).

Canadian, British, and other railway securities.

Call loans on bonds and stocks.

Current loans.

Loans to the Government of Canada.

Loans to provincial governments.

Overdue debts.

Real estate, the property of the bank (other than the bank premises).

Mortgages on real estate sold by the bank.

Bank premises.

Other assets not included under the foregoing heads.

Aggregate amount of loans to directors and firms of which they are partners.

Average amount of specie held during the month.

Average amount of Dominion notes held during the month.

Greatest amount of notes in circulation at any time during the month.

LIABILITIES—*Continued*

To the Public

Deposits, payable on demand or after notice, or on a fixed day, made by other banks in Canada.

Balances due to other banks in Canada in daily exchanges.

Balances due to agencies of the bank, or to other banks or agencies in foreign countries.

Balances due to agencies of the bank, or to other banks or agencies in United Kingdom.

Liabilities not included under foregoing heads.

To the Shareholders

Capital authorized.

Capital subscribed.

Capital paid up.

Amount of rest or reserve fund.

Rate per cent. of last dividend declared.

The publication of the statement first appears in the official gazette and it is immediately thereafter republished, in whole or in part, by almost all the financial journals, while the changes indicating the conditions of finance and trade are commented on by all important daily newspapers. As the banks are few in number and possess extended interests both as to geographical territory and capital employed, they live at all times in the keen sunlight of publicity. In any event, with the information given in such a manner that comparison between one bank and another may be made without effort, it would be hopeless to expect to conceal general weakness, no matter how much it might be concealed in detail.

Under Section 86 the Minister of Finance is given wide powers in order that he may obtain any information he desires from a bank should he suspect weakness in its position or inaccuracy in its monthly returns.

The list of shareholders required under Section 87 is not by any means a perfunctory matter. The information when obtained from all banks is published in a blue-book and is at least examined by many investors who try to judge by the changes from year to year as to the estimation in which certain banks are held.

In accordance with a policy gradually being recognised throughout the world, an addition was made in the act of 1890 by which banks are required to report to Government the unclaimed moneys in their hands (Section 88). These statements also appear in a blue-book for the information of the public.

INSOLVENCY OF BANKS.

The first of the insolvency clauses is that fixing the double liability (Section 89), while Sections 92, 93, 94 and 96 are devoted to elaborate provisions for enforcing it. It will be remembered that the early banks in old Canada had no provision for a double liability of shareholders, but that the charter of the Bank of Nova Scotia (1832) contained the provision, while the Committee for Trade recommended its adoption by old Canada, and long before confederation (1867) it was recognized as a principle.

There was a time when many doubted the practical value of the power to call on shareholders in the event of failure for a second payment to the extent of the face value of their shares. Questionable things were done without hesitation to avoid paying, and many in earlier days could not pay. Shares were transferred by the knowing ones just before failure to others who were, perhaps, incompetent to contract or from whom money could not be collected. Or it was found that the real holder was already a debtor to the bank and could not meet this in addition to his other liabilities. But we have, of late years, had failures in which every species of bad management and misrepresentation has occurred, yet the percentage of the double liability collected has prevented the creditors from suffering. Indeed the conditions laid down by the act make it almost impossible to avoid payment for any reason except inability. Section 90 was inserted in the act of 1890 in order to make it clear that the statute of limitation does not run in favor of a bank in the matter of dividends and deposits. The principle of Section 91 was suggested by the Committee for Trade owing to the difficulty of determining what constituted insolvency in a bank; otherwise, a bank might remain for an indefinite time in the state of suspension.

OFFENCES AND PENALTIES

A careful perusal of the actual text of the act will show that it bristles with penalties, both in the shape of fines and imprisonment. In enforcing promptitude in making returns they are certainly effective, and the enormous fines under Section 51 for over-issues of circulation will doubtless be sufficient for the purpose.

Section 100, the principle of which was introduced in 1880, is intended to prevent private bankers from using titles which might convey the idea of incorporation. In common with many other details of the act, it was borrowed from the United States. The remaining sections of the act are likely to be without interest to the reader.

GENERAL REMARKS ON THE ACT

In dealing with the features of the act which are not disclosed in merely commenting upon its main sections, the Author feels that he cannot do better than repeat, with little alteration, portions of an address to the Congress of Bankers at Chicago, delivered in June, 1893; which was itself based largely upon a pamphlet by the writer, published in 1890, as a defence of the Canadian banking system, regarding which it was feared attempts would be made to assimilate it to the National Banking System of the United States.

What is necessary in a banking system in order that it may answer the requirements of a rapidly growing country and yet be safe and profitable?

1. It should create a currency free from doubt as to value, readily convertible into specie, and answering in volume to the requirements of trade.

2. It should possess the machinery necessary to distribute money over the whole area of the country, so that the smallest possible inequalities in the rate of interest may be the result.

3. It should supply the legitimate wants of the borrower, not merely under ordinary circumstances, but in times of financial stress, at least without that curtailment which leads to abnormal rates of interest and to failures.

4. It should afford the greatest possible measure of safety to the depositor.

NOTE ISSUES

In Canada, as in the United States, the resulting difference in business transactions, after cheques and all other modern instruments of credit have been used, is almost entirely paid in paper money. It is therefore of the greatest importance that the amount of this paper money existing at any one time shall be as nearly as possible just sufficient for the purpose That is, that there shall be a power to issue such money when it is required, and also a power to force it back for redemption when it is not required.

It may therefore, we think, be safely asserted that: (1) There should be as complete a relation as possible between the currency requirements of trade and whatever are the causes which bring about the issue of paper money; (2) and, as it is quite as necessary that no over-issue should be possible as that the supply of currency should be adequate, there should be a similar relation between the requirements of trade and the causes which *force notes back* for redemption.

Now, certainly, one of the *causes* of the issue of bank notes is the profit to be derived therefrom, and it is clear that an amount sufficient for the needs of trade will not be issued unless it is profitable to issue. Likewise it is clear that it should not be possible to keep notes out for the sake of the profit if they are not needed.

In Canada, bank notes, as we have seen, are secured by a first lien upon the entire assets of the bank, including the double liability, the security being general and not special—not, for instance, by the deposit of Government bonds. Therefore it is clear that it will always pay Canadian banks to issue currency when trade demands it. Because bank notes in Canada are issued against the general estate of the bank, they are subject to *actual* daily redemption; and no bank dares to issue notes without reference to its power to redeem, any more than a solvent merchant dares to give promissory notes without reference to his ability to pay. The presentation for actual redemption of every note not required for purposes of trade is assured by the fact that every bank seeks by the activity of its own business to keep out its own notes, and therefore sends back daily for redemption the notes of all other banks. This great feature in the Canadian system, as compared with the National Banking System, is generally overlooked, but it is because of this actual daily redemption that there has never been any serious inflation of the currency, if indeed there has ever been inflation at all. Trade, of course, becomes inflated, and the currency will follow trade, but that is a very different thing from the existence in a country of a great volume of paper money not required by trade. It is hardly necessary to discuss at length this quality of elasticity in the system, because it is generally admitted. But some critic may endeavor to show that a similar quality might be given to a currency secured by Government bonds, and it may be well to make it clear that such elasticity as is required in North America is impossible with a currency secured by Government bonds. In the older countries of the world it may be sufficient if the volume of currency rises and falls with the general course of trade over a series of years, and without reference to the fluctuations within the twelve months of the year. In North America it is not enough that the volume of currency should rise and fall from year to year. In Canada we find that between the low average of the circulation during about eight months of each year and the maximum attained at the busiest period of the autumn and winter there is a difference of twenty per cent., the movement upward in the autumn and downward in the spring being so sudden, that without the power in the banks to issue, in the autumn serious stringency must result, and without the force which brings about redemption in the spring there must be plethora. As a matter of fact, it works automatically, and there is always enough and never too much.

If the currency were secured by Government bonds, the volume in existence at any one time would be determined by the profit to be gained by the issue of such bond-secured currency. It would, therefore, be necessary to fix a maximum beyond which no currency could be issued, but as such an arbitrary limit would be mere legislative guess-work, it would be productive of the evils incident to all efforts to curb natural laws by legislation. As we know, when the National Bank charters were offered by the Federal Government to the State banks, the bonds of the United States bore five to six per cent. interest, and the business of issuing currency against such bonds was so profitable that a maximum such as that referred to was fixed, with an elaborate provision stating how the banking charters were to be distributed as to area, in order that each State or section of country might have a fair share. This was followed by several adjustments, the last limit fixed was $354,000,000, all who wished the privilege were dissatisfied with the limitation of issues, and the cry of monopoly was frequently heard. Subsequently the attempt to fix a maximum was abandoned; indeed, the business of issuing notes against Government bonds had become unprofitable, and there was no longer any fear of inflation.

The condition in the United States under which the issue of currency was unduly profitable, and the fear of inflation was present, did not actually last many years, but it lasted long enough to create in the people a hatred of banks which does not seem yet to have passed away. The condition which followed showed conclusively, it seems to me, the unsoundness of the system in the matter of providing an elastic currency—a currency *at all times* adequate in volume. The currency wants of the country increased with the great increase in business and population, but the volume of National Bank currency decreased, because by the repayment of the national debt and the improvement in the national credit the bonds which remained outstanding yielded so low a rate of interest as to make the issue of National Bank notes unprofitable.

The writer hopes he has made it clear that if the business of issuing currency against Government bonds were profitable, too much currency would be the result; and if it were unprofitable, too little would be issued. We would require to have a condition of things under which the profit of issuing notes would at all times bear an exact relation to the amount of currency required by the country, the profit therefore changing not only as the currency rises and falls over a series of years, but at the time of the sharp fluctuations within each year, already referred to. No such relation, however, could very well exist with an issue based upon Government bonds.

The next quality in a currency to be considered is that it should be readily convertible into specie. We do not propose to discuss this at length. The assurance of convertibility lies in the actual daily redemption to which we have referred. This is the best possible safeguard against suspension of specie payments.

THE BORROWER AND THE BRANCH SYSTEM

In the banking systems of older countries, the borrower is not often considered. Men must borrow where and how they can, and pay as much or as little for the money as circumstances require. We believe too strongly in the necessity for an absolute performance of engagements to think it necessary that any banking system should render the path of the debtor easy. But in America the debtor class is apt to make itself heard, and the writer wishes to show what the branch system, as compared with the United States National Banking System, does for the worthy borrower.

In a country where the money accumulated each year by the people's savings does not exceed the money required for new business ventures, it is plain that that system of banking is the best which most completely gathers up these savings and places them at the disposal of the borrower. This practically means that the savings of slow-going communities are applied to other communities where the enterprise is out of proportion to the money at their own command. In Canada, with its banks with forty and fifty branches, we see the deposits of the saving communities applied directly to the country's new enterprises in a manner nearly perfect. One bank borrows money from depositors at Halifax and many points in the maritime provinces, where the savings largely exceed the new enterprises, and it lends money in Vancouver or in the Northwest, where the new enterprises far exceed the savings. Another in the same manner gathers deposits in the unenterprising parts of Ontario, and lends the money in the enterprising localities of the same. The result is that forty or fifty business centres, in no case having an exact equilibrium of deposits and loans, are able to adjust the excess or deficiency of capital, the depositor obtaining a fair rate of interest, and the borrower obtaining money at a lower rate than borrowers in any of the colonies of Great Britain, and a lower average rate than in the United States, except in the very great cities in the East. So perfectly is this distribution of capital made, that as between the highest class borrower in Montreal or Toronto and the merchant in the Northwest, the difference in interest paid is not more than one to two per cent.

In the United States, banks have no branches. There are banks in New York and the East seeking investment for their money, and refusing to allow any interest because there are not sufficient borrowers to take up their deposits; and there are banks in the West and South which cannot begin to supply their borrowing customers, because they have only the money of the immediate locality at their command, and have no direct access to the money in the East. To avoid a difficulty which would otherwise be unbearable, the Western and Southern banks sometimes rediscount their customers' notes with banks in the East, while many of their customers, not being able to rely upon them for assistance, are forced to float paper through Eastern note-brokers. But the Western and Southern banks wanting money, and the Eastern banks having it, cannot come together by chance, and there is no satisfactory machinery for bringing them together. So it follows that a Boston bank may be anxiously looking for investments at four or five per cent., while in some rich Western State ten and even twelve per cent. is being paid. These are extreme cases, but we have quoted an extreme case in Canada, where the capital marches automatically across the Continent to find the borrower, and the extra interest obtained scarcely pays the loss of time it would take to send it so far were the machinery not so perfect.

As we have indicated, it should be the object of every country to so distribute loanable capital that every borrower with adequate security can be reached by someone able to lend, and the machinery for doing this has always been recognized in the banks. That is surely not a good system of banking under which the surplus money in every unenterprising community has a tendency to stay there, while the surplus money required by an enterprising community has to be sought at a distance. If by paying a higher rate of interest, and seeking diligently, it could always be found, the position would not be so bad. The fact is that when it is most wanted, distrust is at its height, and the cautious banker buttons up his pocket. When there is no inducement to avert trouble to a community by supplying its wants in time of financial stress, there is no inclination to do so. Banks with small capital and no branches are not apt to have a very large sense of responsibility for the welfare of the country as a whole, or for any considerable portion of it. But the banks in Canada, with thirty, forty, or fifty branches, with interests which it is no exaggeration to describe as national, cannot be idle or indifferent in time of trouble, cannot turn a deaf ear to the legitimate wants of the farmer in the prairie provinces, any more than to the wealthy merchant or manufacturer in the East. Their business is to gather up the wealth of a nation, not of a town or city, and to supply the borrowing wants of a nation.

There was a time in Canada, about twenty years ago, when some people thought that in every town, a bank, no matter how small, provided it had no branches, and had its owners resident in the neighborhood, was a greater help to the town than the branch of a large and powerful bank. In those days, perhaps, the great banks were too autocratic, had not been taught by competition to respect fully the wants of each community. If this feeling existed to any extent, it has passed away. We are, in fact, in danger of the results of over-competition. There are, indeed, few countries in the world so well supplied with banking facilities as Canada. The branch system not only enables every town of 1,000 or 1,200 people to have a joint-stock bank, but to have a bank with a power behind it generally twenty to fifty times greater than a bank would have such as is found in towns of similar size in the United States.

THE DEPOSITOR

The legal position of the depositor is about the same in Canada as it is in the United States. The note-holder's claim is preferred to his. We must not, however, expect that any government will relieve a depositor from the necessity of using discretion as to where he places his money. Governments never have done and never can do that. Men must use their intelligence, and after measuring the security offered, judge where they should intrust their money. It is perhaps easier for a man with limited intelligence to make a selection if the banks have large capital and are of semi-national importance, provided, of course, the basis of the system is not unsound, as it is, for example, in Italy and Australia. In Canada, we do not obtain deposits from abroad, although we might not object to do so if money could be obtained at low enough rates of interest; and we do not lend on real estate, as banks do in Australia. The Government statement of March 31, 1894, shows that before depositors having claims amounting to $187,000,000 can suffer, shareholders must lose in paid-up stock and double liability as much as $125,000,000, and $26,000,000 of surplus funds; in all, $151,000,000. There are probably few countries in the world where greater security is offered to depositors.

When the bank charters were under discussion in 1890, the writer had occasion to make publicly a statement which, in view of the several failures of branch banks in Australia since, might now excite more criticism than it did then. In making a comparison between individual banks with small capital and banks with branches and large capital, it was urged that "the probability of loss to the depositors in one bank with several millions of capital is less than the probability of loss to some of the depositors in ten or twenty small banks having in the aggregate the same capital and deposits as the large bank."

The retort will be quickly made, "But if the large bank fails, the ruin will be just so much the more widespread."

This is quite true, but it is not an answer to the point, although it may appear to be so. If the conditions of two countries are about the same, and the ability of the bankers and the principles of the banking system are in other respects equally excellent, it must still remain true that the probability of loss to some of the depositors in the ten or twenty small banks is greater than the probability of loss to any of the depositors in the one large bank.

In the closing chapter, a statement of the failures of banks in Canada since confederation in 1867 is given, and from this the loss to depositors may be estimated.

BANK INSPECTION

We have in Canada no public bank examiner as in the United States, nor are the annual statements of banks audited as in Australia. When the audit system was proposed by the Government, the bankers resisted because they felt that it pretended to protect the shareholders and creditors, but did not really do so. If an audit would not really protect the shareholders and creditors, it seemed better that they should not be lulled by imaginary safeguards, but be kept alert by the constant exercise of their own judgment. So far as the bankers have ever discussed with the Government the question of public bank examiners, they have confined their arguments to pointing out the impracticability when banks have many branches. This may, in the minds of some, constitute an argument against branch banking. We simply state the facts.

But bankers say that while it might be very well to have public examiners for the protection of the people—if it really would lessen bank failures—it is much more necessary with branch banking to have bank examiners, or, as they are called, inspectors, on behalf of the executive of the bank. When it comes to the quality of the work done by such trained inspectors, it would not be too much to assert that it is almost certain to be better than that of a public official. In the larger banks the inspection staff consists of several men who are actively engaged for the whole year in completing one tour of the branches. Some of these officers devote themselves to the routine of the branches, verifying the cash, securities, bills, accounts, etc., testing the compliance of officers with the regulations of the bank, reporting on the skill and character of officers, etc., while the chiefs devote themselves to the higher matters, such as the quality of the bills under discount, loans against securities—indeed, the quality and value of *every* asset at the branch. They also deal with the growth and profitableness of the branch, its prospects, etc. These matters have already passed the judgment of the branch manager, and the more important have been referred to and approved by the executive, so that it may be said that three different judgments are passed upon the business of the branch. But it will be said that the chief inspector may be under the sway of the executive and his reports a mere echo of the opinion of the latter. This is quite true—the reports may be dishonest. Our bankers do not tell the public that the inspector is specially employed for its protection. He, like the general manager, is merely a part of the bank's machinery for conducting its business, and the public is left to judge of the bank by its chief officers, its record in the past, its *entourage*.

CHAPTER VI

LAND BANKS—LOAN COMPANIES

SAVINGS-BANKS—DOMINION NOTES—BANK FAILURES

NO account of the joint-stock banks alone would constitute an adequate study of the banking of a country, yet it is impossible in this work to make more than the briefest mention of the land banks or building and loan companies and the savings-banks of Canada. A very complete account has, however, just been published in the third volume of the "Journal of the Canadian Bankers' Association," page 227, entitled "The Land Mortgage Companies, Government Savings-Banks, and Private Bankers of Canada," by Massey Morris. From this we learn that the total banking assets of Canada, excluding private bankers, at the nearest date convenient for Mr. Morris' purposes, were as follows:

Chartered banks—Total assets (1893)		$304,363,580
Loan companies—Total assets (1893)		133,250,285
Government—Legal-tender notes in circulation	1893 $18,448,494	
Government—Savings-bank deposits	41,849,658	
		60,298,152
Quebec savings-banks—Total assets (April, 1895)		15,307,637
Total............		$513,219,654

LAND MORTGAGE COMPANIES

The history of land mortgage companies in Canada dates back a little more than fifty years, the first legislation occurring apparently in Upper Canada (Ontario), in which province alone the system has largely developed. It is, however, clearly destined to have a large development in the new provinces of the Northwest. That the growth of this form of money-lending has been rapid is indicated by the fact that while the total loans in 1874 were only about $15,000,000, in 1893 they had reached $115,000,000. By a statement given later it will be seen that this growth is almost entirely in Ontario. Unfortunately, there is no general act, as in commercial banking, to which all must conform, and no single source of authority. Charters are granted both by the Dominion and Provincial Governments, while there are five companies working under Imperial charters, there being nothing to prevent foreign corporations from doing business in the country. As a consequence, complete statements are not yet placed before the public, although great efforts are made by the Dominion Government and that of the province of Ontario to obtain returns showing the operations of the companies. When Mr. Morris wrote the article referred to, he had before him a return to the Dominion Government covering the names of eighty-two companies, while another to the province of Ontario covered eighty-six. There are doubtless altogether not as many as one hundred companies, counting every variety, doing business in the Dominion. For the reasons given, there is considerable incongruity in the powers accorded to the various companies, and it is not easy to state the principles which actuated the different governments in granting charters. A few leading features, however, may be indicated. Loans must be confined to real property and bonds, stocks, and similar collaterals. There is a limit in proportion to capital to the amount of liability which may be incurred, although no settled rule prevails. There is no double liability resting upon the stockholders. The weakest feature is the permission to many companies to accept deposits which are practically repayable on demand. It must be clear that if a commercial bank whose deposits are repayable on demand, or on short notice, is restrained by law from lending on real property, a company lending on real property should be restrained from accepting deposits repayable on demand. Public opinion is moving rapidly in this direction, and many companies have as a matter of policy and wisdom withdrawn from acquiring deposits except in exchange for the time debentures of the company.

Thus far, the record of the land mortgage companies in Canada is excellent. Very few have failed, and in no instance have the creditors not been paid in full.

A statement taken from the article referred to is appended, to show the volume of business as far as it is disclosed by the imperfect returns at the Author's disposal. The reader's attention is drawn to the fact that while the deposits of Canadian banks are all practically made by Canadians, the land mortgage companies have, out of deposits amounting to about $80,000,000, borrowed about $50,000,000 in foreign countries, which, in the main, means Scotland.

LIABILITIES, BY PROVINCES, FOR THE YEAR 1893 (CENTS OMITTED)

Provinces	Number of Companies	Capital Stock Subscribed	Capital Stock Fully Paid Up	Amount Paid on Capital Stock Not Fully Paid Up	Accumulating Stock	Reserve Fund	Dividends Declared and Unpaid	Profits on Accumulating Stock	Contingent Fund and Unappropriated Profits	Liabilities to Stockholders
Ontario	71	$87,345,402	$18,985,228	$13,980,683	$690,732	$10,397,000	$989,488	$46,873	$949,356	$86,039,363
Quebec.....	8	6,220,249	955,960	1,422,880	86,057	523,855	47,265	19,152	219,151	3,274,321
Nova Scotia	2	201,000	....	100,500	616,548	10,000	2,513	......	4,646	734,207
Grand Total	81	$93,766,651	$19,941,188	$15,504,063	$1,393,337	$10,930,896	$1,039,266	$66,025	$1,173,155	$90,047,892

Provinces	Deposits	Debentures Payable in Canada	Debentures Payable Elsewhere	Debenture Stock	Interest on Deposits, Debentures and Debenture Stock	Owing to Banks	Other Liabilities	Liabilities to the Public	Total Liabilities
Ontario...........	$17,932,089	$9,353,629	$42,942,963	$2,613,395	$790,265	$162,764	$661,006	$74,698,113	$120,697,477
Quebec...........	477,230	470,372	6,465,435	....	18,041	......	144,241	7,375,306	10,649,643
Nova Scotia	122,253	202,100	....	....	4,254	......	500	329,108	1,063,315
Grand Total	$18,531,573	$10,028,102	$49,408,398	$2,613,395	$812,562	$162,764	$805,748	$82,362,544	$132,410,436

Liabilities of the Scottish-American Investment Company (Limited) not included.

ASSETS, BY PROVINCES, FOR THE YEAR 1893 (CENTS OMITTED)

Provinces	Number of Companies	A—Current Loans Secured on							Otherwise Secured	Total	B—Property Owned	
		Real Estate	Dominion Securities	County or City Securities	Township, Town or Village Securities	School Section Securities	Loan Comp'nies' Debentures	Loans to Shareholders on their Stock			Dominion Securities	Provincial Securities
Ontario..........	72	$100,782,388	$......	$276,478	$232,163	$8,493	$17,174	$671,214	$3,042,942	$105,030,856	$354,910	$26,553
Quebec..........	8	9,152,712	......	......	1,000	......	......	82,934	90,431	9,327,079	......	244,828
Nova Scotia......	2	981,458	......	......	......	......	......	......	7,391	988,850	......	......
Total.........	82	$110,916,559	......	$276,478	$233,163	$8,493	$17,174	$754,149	$3,140,766	$115,346,786	$354,910	$271,381

Provinces	B—Property Owned										Total Assets
	County or City Securities	Township, Town, or Village Securities	School Section Securities	Loan Comp'nies' Debentures	Office Furniture and Fixtures	Cash on Hand	Cash in Banks	Office Premises	Loans Secured on Real Estate Held for Sale	Other Property	Total Property Owned	
Ontario.....	$1,016,160	$694,211	$197,877	$236,011	$41,835	$84,077	$2,024,004	$1,476,513	$3,298,424	$7,101,148	$16,506,469	$121,537,325
Quebec.....	....	......	......	......	915	2,983	616,208	32,636	27,533	397,459	1,312,564	10,649,643
Nova Scotia.	....	......	......	......	410	75	2,407	8,609	17,726	45,237	74,465	1,063,315
Total....	$1,016,160	$694,211	$197,877	$236,011	$43,160	$87,136	$2,642,619	$1,517,759	$3,343,684	$7,543,845	$17,903,499	$133,250,285

SAVINGS-BANKS

In considering the savings-banks of Canada it is first necessary to bear in mind that they represent the savings to a moderate extent only of those who have money upon which they desire to earn interest, but which they prefer to intrust to a bank rather than invest in a specific security; in other words, the savings-bank class of depositors. Upon deposits of this class, no matter how small in amount, the ordinary Canadian banks are prepared to pay interest, and the banks, with few exceptions, have what are called savings-bank departments. Without estimating what proportion of the total deposits in the ordinary banks is of this character, it would be impossible to make use of the figures as evidence of the saving habits of the people.

Before confederation there were a few incorporated savings-banks in Lower Canada (Quebec) and Upper Canada (Ontario), but in the maritime provinces Government savings-banks had been established; not, however, on the plan of the post-office savings-banks of Great Britain. When the first Finance Ministers of the new Dominion came to face their financial difficulties, one of the expedients resorted to, in addition to the issue of legal tenders, was the establishment of post-office savings-banks, in the main following the plan in force in Great Britain. The Government also took over the provincial savings-banks already in operation in the maritime provinces, and it still carries on the two systems of savings-banks, although they are gradually being merged into a uniform post-office system. The incorporated savings-banks in the meantime have either taken on the powers of land mortgage banks or have practically disappeared, with the exception of two powerful institutions in Quebec, one at Montreal and one at Quebec City. We append a table taken from Mr. Morris' article, which shows at once the growth since confederation and the division between the three classes of savings-banks. The third column consists almost entirely of the deposits of the two incorporated savings-banks in the province of Quebec already mentioned :

Year Ended June 30th.	Post-office Savings-banks.	Other Government Savings-banks.	Special Savings-banks.	Totals.
1868............	$204,589	$1,683,219	$3,369,799	$5,057,607
1869............	856,814	1,694,525	3,960,818	6,412,157
1870............	1,588,849	1,822,570	5,369,103	8,780,522
1871............	2,497,260	2,072,037	5,766,712	10,336,009
1872............	3,096,500	2,154,233	5,557,126	10,807,859
1873............	3,207,052	2,958,170	6,768,662	12,933,884
1874............	3,204,965	4,005,296	6,811,009	14,021,270
1875............	2,926,090	4,245,091	6,611,416	13,782,579
1876............	2,740,952	4,303,166	6,519,229	13,563,347
1877............	2,639,937	4,830,694	6,054,456	13,525,087
1878............	2,754,484	5,742,529	5,631,172	14,128,185
1879............	3,105,191	6,102,492	5,494,164	14,701,847
1880............	3,945,669	7,107,287	6,681,025	17,733,981
1881............	6,208,227	9,628,445	7,685,888	23,522,560
1882............	9,473,661	12,295,001	8,658,435	30,427,096
1883............	11,976,237	14,242,870	8,791,045	35,010,152
1884............	13,245,553	15,971,983	8,851,142	38,068,679
1885............	15,090,540	17,888,536	9,191,895	42,170,971
1886............	17,159,372	20,014,442	9,177,132	46,350,946
1887............	19,497,750	21,334,525	10,092,143	50,924,418
1888............	20,689,033	20,682,025	10,475,292	51,846,350
1889............	23,011,423	19,944,934	10,761,061	53,717,419
1890............	21,990,653	19,021,812	10,908,987	51,921,452
1891............	21,738,648	17,661,378	10,982,232	50,382,258
1892............	22,298,402	17,231,146	12,236,100	51,765,648
1893............	24,153,194	17,696,464	12,823,836	54,673,494

Whether the plan is destined to be permanent which was first adopted in Great Britain, and which has now spread to so many countries, of the Government taking the money of the people and allowing interest thereon, is beyond the scope of our inquiry. It has involved Great Britain in many very serious difficulties, and it cannot fail to cause considerable trouble to any government which endeavors by such means to occupy the place of bankers. But in Canada the reason moving the Finance Minister in 1867 was not philanthropical—he merely wanted money—and for many years it was a means of borrowing from the people—the rate of interest being higher than first-class banks could afford to pay. Even now, the rate paid is three and a half per cent. per annum, which is higher than the rate ordinarily paid by banks. For this rate no justification can be found. The Government is now in the highest grade of credit among British dependencies, and only two or three nations in the world can borrow at lower rates of interest, so that when to three and a half per cent. per annum is added the cost of maintaining about forty special offices and of gathering money at over 700 post-offices, the rate cannot be justified by any argument based upon the mere value of money. Theoretically, the intelligent and well-to-do are not supposed to take advantage of this species of public bonus given to encourage habits of saving, and of this paternal care intended to avert loss to depositors who lack intelligence. Therefore there is a limit ($1000) to the amount to be deposited in any single year, and another limit ($3000) to the total, which may stand at the credit of any one name. When this maximum is reached, however, if the depositor is not clever enough to adopt expedients for depositing his money in the name of another, he can convert his deposit into some other form of Government obligation, such as inscribed stock, and begin to deposit in the savings-bank again.

DOMINION NOTE ISSUES

It will be remembered that when legal-tender notes were authorized, under the Dominion Note Act, to replace those formerly issued under the Provincial Note Act, the limit was placed at $9,000,000, issues in excess being permitted if an equal amount of gold was reserved. From time to time, however, the Government extended the limit of these notes, secured only in part by gold (with a minimum requirement of fifteen per cent. and Government bonds for the balance), until it was fixed at $20,000,000. But while these later issues were partly the result of the increase of the requirements of the country in change-making notes (those of smaller denominations than five dollars), they were mainly caused by the requirements of the banks in notes of large denominations used for making settlements, and therefore the Government found it expedient to keep much larger gold reserves than those named in the act. Now that the issues are likely to exceed considerably the limit of $20,000,000, the act has been amended and the Government has definitely avowed its purpose of keeping an equal amount of gold for all issues in excess of the limit named. With the growth of the change-making notes, which cannot well be presented for redemption on the one hand, and the increasing stock of gold as the issues reach higher figures, almost all danger from this bad system of financing will pass away, and Section 50 will, we hope, some day be removed from the Bank Act.

The statement below shows the amount of notes in circulation at the close of each of the months ending with March 31, 1896. It will be observed that about two-thirds of the entire issue is in large notes used almost alone by banks for settlement purposes. At the request of the banks the Government has consented to issue a special form of legal-tender note, negotiable only between chartered banks, in order to lessen the risk of loss by carrying large amounts to and from the clearing-houses or from bank to bank, and the danger of robbery or fraud in any other manner, always incident to notes payable to bearer. If, as it is hoped by many, this results in the conversion of the major part of the notes of high denominations now payable to bearer into notes only negotiable between banks, it will be made evident to all that the functions of the Dominion Note Act are sharply separated under two heads.

1st. To provide for the community, including the banks, the change-making notes required for the transaction of the business operations of the country, of which at any one time no considerable proportion could be presented for redemption.

2nd. To issue notes of large denominations, almost all of which are held by the banks.

	1895 31st October	1895 30th November	1895 31st December	1896 31st January	1896 29th February	1896 31st March
Fractionals	$202,311 25	$202,276 25	$221,855 25	$221,437 25	$222,096 75	$203,616 75
$1 and $2	7,312,917 00	7,325,053 00	7,217,448 00	6,739,916 00	6,653,915 90	6,[illegible] 50
$4	375,180 00	375,176 00	364,664 00	330,848 00	337,236 00	344,[illegible] 00
$5, $10 and $20	8,845 37	8,845 37	8,845 37	8,845 37	8,840 37	8,835 37
$50 and $100	248,100 00	242,450 00	254,150 00	235,250 00	210,250 00	209,190 00
$500 and $1,000	14,746,000 00	14,704,500 00	14,398,900 00	12,148,000 00	11,440,000 00	11,398,500 00
Total	$22,893,259 62	$22,878,300 62	$22,413,462 62	$19,684,276 62	$18,872,358 62	$18,791,749 62

Fractional notes	$203,616 75
Provincial notes	29,512 87
Dominion ones and twos	6,989,438 00
Dominion fours	344,[illegible] 00
Montreal large notes	5,990,100 00
Toronto "	3,346,400 00
Halifax "	690,500 00
St. John "	1,089,500 00
Winnipeg "	177,000 00
Charlottetown "	146,000 00
Victoria "	216,000 00
Total	$18,791,749 62

Specie held by the several Assistant Receivers-General on the 31st March, 1896	$7,049,897 33
Guaranteed sterling debentures, £400,000 sterling	1,946,666 67
Total	$8,996,564 00
Specie and guaranteed debentures to be held under the Revised Statutes of Canada, cap. 31, as amended by 58-59 Vic., cap. 16—25 per cent. on $18,791,749.62	4,697,937 40
Excess of specie and guaranteed debentures	$4,298,626 60
Unguaranteed debentures	$17,250,000 00
Unguaranteed debentures to be held under the Revised Statutes of Canada, cap. 31, as amended by 58-59 Vic., cap. 16—75 per cent. on $18,791,749.62	14,093,812 22
Excess of unguaranteed debentures	$3,156,187 78

SUMMARY

Excess of specie and guaranteed sterling debentures	$4,298,626 60
" unguaranteed debentures	3,156,187 78
Total excess	$7,454,814 38

Insolvent Banks and those having gone into Liquidation Since Confederation, 1867

Name of Bank and Place of Head Office	Date of Charter	Date of Suspension	Capital Stock at Date of Suspension: Capital Subscribed	Capital Stock at Date of Suspension: Capital Paid Up	Total Assets at date of Suspension	Total Liabilities at date of Suspension	Dividends Paid: Note-holders	Dividends Paid: Depositors
							Per cent.	Per cent.
1. Commercial Bank of New Brunswick, St. John	Local, before confederation	Last ret'n July, '68	$600,000	$600,000	$1,222,454	$671,420	In full	In full
2. Bank of Acadia, Liverpool, N.S.	35 Vic., ch. 55, June 14, 1872	April, 1873	500,000	100,000	213,346	106,914	......	......
3. Metropolitan Bank, Montreal	34 Vic., ch. 39, April 14, 1871	Winding-up Act passed 40 Vic., ch. 56 (1877), ret'n Oct. 1876	1,000,000	800,170	779,225	293,379	In full	In full
4. Mechanics' Bank, Montreal	Before confederation	May, 1879	243,374	194,794	721,155	547,238	57⅛	57⅛
5. Consolidated Bank, Montreal	Sept. 18, 1875, by amalgamation of City Bank and Royal Canadian, 69 Vic., ch. 44	August, 1879	2,091,900	2,080,920	3,077,202	1,794,249	In full	In full
6. Bank of Liverpool, Liverpool, N.S.	34 Vic., ch. 42, April 14, 1871	October, 1879	500,000	470,548	207,877	136,480	"	......
7. Stadacona Bank, Quebec	35 Vic., ch. 58, June 14, 1872	Voluntary liquidation July, '79 Winding-up Act, 43 Vic., ch. 48 (1880)	1,000,000	991,890	1,335,675	341,500	"	In full
8. Exchange Bank of Canada, Montreal	34 Vic., ch. 42, April 14, 1871	September, 1883	500,000	500,000	3,335,907	2,431,935	"	66½
9. Maritime Bank of the Dominion of Canada, St. John, N.B.	35 Vic., ch. 58, June 14, 1872	March, 1887	321,900	321,900	1,825,993	1,409,482	"	10 6-10
10. Pictou Bank, Pictou, N.S.	36 Vic., ch. 76, May 23, 1873	Under Act 50 Vic., ch. 54, Sep. '87	500,000	200,000	277,017	74,364	"	In full
11. Bank of London in Canada, London, Ont.	46 Vic., ch. 52, May 25, 1883	August, 1887	1,000,000	241,101	1,132,118	838,330	"	"
12. Central Bank of Canada, Toronto	46 Vic., ch. 50, May 25, 1883	November, 1887	500,000	500,000	3,231,518	2,631,378	"	99⅔
13. Federal Bank of Canada, Toronto; changed from the "Superior Bank of Canada"	35 Vic., ch. 59, 36 Vic., ch. 5, 37 Vic., ch. 57, May 26, '74	Vol'tary liquidation Jan., 1888.	1,250,000	1,250,000	4,869,113	3,449,499	"	In full
14. Bank of Prince Ed. Isl'd, Charlottetown, P.E.I.	Local charter by Prov'l Gov.	November, 1881	......	......	......	......	......	......
15. Commercial Bank of Manitoba	47 Vic., ch. 50, April 19, 1894	June 30, 1893	740,700	552,650	1,951,151	1,341,251	In full	80 to date
16. Banque du Peuple	7 Vic., ch. 66, June 27, 1844	July 15, 1895	*1,200,000	1,200,000	8,163,308	6,820,450	"	......

* The figures for the Banque du Peuple are as at July 31, 1895, sixteen days after actual date of suspension. The notes in circulation at the time of preparing this statement (May, [illegible]) had been reduced below the sum ([illegible]) held by the Government as the share of the Bank Circulation Redemption Fund deposited by the Banque du Peuple, and which will be returnable to the failed bank proportionately as the remaining notes are redeemed. For this reason we have referred to the bank in the above statement as having paid its note-holders in full.

17 Banque de Ville Marie 1900

BANK FAILURES

Although we have not been able to follow in detail the incidents showing the growth and fortunes of banking since confederation, we present in the preceding table a statement of the bank failures during the period 1867 to 1896.

Leaving out of consideration the Bank of Prince Edward Island, the provincial charter of which had not expired when it suspended, and which was not therefore a bank doing business under the Dominion Act, we find that out of fifteen failures, nine banks paid both note-holders and ordinary creditors in full, and four more paid note-holders in full. Of the four who paid note-holders in full, but not ordinary creditors, one, the Commercial Bank of Manitoba, has paid eighty per cent. to ordinary creditors, and is still in process of liquidation. Another, the Central Bank of Canada, paid to ordinary creditors all but one-third of one cent in the dollar, and would certainly have paid all claims in full had not the liquidators been allowed quite too large fees for their services. A third, the Banque du Peuple, is now being liquidated, and it would not be proper for the writer to express at the present time an opinion as to the dividend the ordinary creditors are likely to receive. The point to be observed is, that it is a bank with an abnormal charter, under which there is no double liability on the part of the stockholders, although there is an unlimited liability on the part of the directors, and the results of its failure do not concern us in estimating the value of the present system. The remaining bank, which paid its note-holders but not its ordinary creditors, was the Maritime Bank of St. John, N.B. Its record is very bad. The claims of the Dominion and Provincial Governments, which rank next to the note-holders', were paid in full, but the ordinary creditors received only 10.60 per cent. of their claims. The double liability failed to produce one-half of the face value of the shares at the time of suspension.

We have now left for consideration two banks which have paid neither note-holders nor ordinary creditors in full, and the fact that note-holders were not paid is, of course, of prime importance. Whatever care it may be possible for the State to take for the protection of depositors, no system, so far as the writer is aware, professes to do so absolutely, while it may be asserted that no system approaches perfection which does not absolutely protect the note-holder. The two failures referred to took place at a time when the notes were not a first lien on the estate of the bank, although it will be remembered that the bankers had suggested that the law be so made. When the Mechanics' Bank was wound up, only fifty-seven and one-half per cent. was paid to note-holders and other creditors, and at the next revision of the act the change referred to was made. The other, the Bank of Acadia, has been described as a fraudulent affair, and it stands out conspicuously as an evidence of the value of two features of the present act—that a new bank shall have a sufficiently large capital to make it reasonably clear that it is a *bona fide* venture, and that the capital in actual cash shall be paid into the office of the Finance Minister before permission to begin business is granted. This bank had nominally a capital of $500,000 subscribed, and $100,000 paid up, but there appears to have been no real capital, or practically none. It existed for four or five months, paying a commission to float its notes, and then failed. Its notes had been redeemed by a bank correspondent, but to what extent they were in circulation at the moment of failure, or whether any dividend was paid, the writer, after several efforts, cannot learn.

To sum up the evidence from the foregoing facts, it appears that if the Bank Act had assumed its present shape at the time of confederation no holder of a Canadian bank note would have suffered loss.

RETURNS TO GOVERNMENT

We will now close this study of Canadian Banking by appending a copy of the latest Government return, in the form in which it is condensed for the readers of the "Journal of the Canadian Bankers' Association." The writer once more expresses the hope that the comparatively unimportant scope of Canadian banking will not cause any reader to lay less stress upon the principles set forth. It does not, however, follow that a system of banking which suits admirably the environment in which it is placed can be transplanted. In banking, the most cherished dogma of one country may be rank heresy in another. The main point is that the Canadian banker has spent his energy to make perfect that which he had, rather than to

"Seek painted trifles and fantastic toys,
And eagerly pursue imaginary joys."

and that the people of Canada are satisfied that the result is good.

Statement of Banks Acting Under Dominion Government Charter for the Month ending March 31, [illegible].

LIABILITIES

	March, [illegible]	March, [illegible]
Capital authorised	$ 73,458,[illegible]5	$ 73,4[illegible]
Capital paid up	61,[illegible]	[illegible]
Reserve fund	27,390,674	[illegible]
Notes in circulation	$ [illegible],414,796	$ 30,[illegible]457
Dominion and Provincial Government deposits	9,543,430	6,[illegible]
Public deposits on demand	63,452,[illegible]	[illegible]
Public deposits after notice	1[illegible]4,417,[illegible]	120,[illegible]
Bank loans or deposits from other banks, secured	80,153	20,500
Bank loans or deposits from other banks, unsecured	2,791,[illegible]	2,[illegible]
Due other banks in Canada in daily exchanges	120,815	83,[illegible]
Due other banks in foreign countries	167,[illegible]5	135,[illegible]17
Due other banks in Great Britain	4,137,[illegible]	5,[illegible]
Other liabilities	[illegible],165	[illegible]
Total liabilities	$224,550,151*	[illegible]

*In this statement the cents are omitted.

ASSETS

Specie	$ 8,058,599	$ 7,797,099
Dominion notes	15,071,091	12,737,996
Deposits to secure note circulation	1,810,736	1,816,011
Notes and cheques of other banks	6,056,477	6,341,636
Loans to other banks, secured	80,153	15,500
Deposits made with other banks	3,284,390	3,273,695
Due from other banks in foreign countries	21,214,061	16,400,267
Due from other banks in Great Britain	4,113,422	4,417,380
Dominion Government debentures or stock	2,685,139	2,991,549
Public, municipal, and railway securities	18,736,605	19,877,893
Call loans on bonds and stocks	17,279,287	13,849,628
Loans to Dominion and Provincial Governments	1,479,932	462,743
Current loans and discounts	199,086,112	211,603,718
Due from other banks in Canada in daily exchanges	136,754	107,153
Overdue debts	3,042,985	4,344,192
Real estate	1,062,473	1,485,358
Mortgages on real estate sold	560,788	582,288
Bank premises	5,510,838	5,655,524
Other assets	2,019,553	1,931,452
Total assets	$311,289,599	$315,691,276

Average amount of specie held during the month	$ 8,050,859	$ 7,780,843
Average Dominion notes held during the month	15,296,161	12,787,159
Loans to directors or their firms	7,653,882	7,936,789
Greatest amount of notes in circulation during month	30,312,847	31,521,232

www.ingramcontent.com/pod-product-compliance
Lightning Source LLC
Chambersburg PA
CBHW031601170426
43196CB00032B/942
* 9 7 8 3 7 4 3 3 1 3 7 6 7 *